Yes! Secrets for Your Best Life – Law of Attraction
plus Hidden Power
Increases Your Success and Happiness

2nd Edition, greatly expanded

Tom Marcoux
America's Communication Coach
TFG Thought Leader
Speaker-Author of 25 books
Blogger, BeHeardandBeTrusted.com

A QuickBreakthrough Publishing Edition

Copyright © 2015 Tom Marcoux Media, LLC
ISBN: 0692330690
ISBN-13: 978-0692330692

All rights reserved. No part of this book may be reproduced or transmitted in any form by any means electronic or mechanical, including photocopying, recording or by any information storage and retrieval system without written permission from the publisher.

QuickBreakthrough Publishing is an imprint of Tom Marcoux Media, LLC. More copies are available from the publisher, Tom Marcoux Media, LLC. Please call (415) 572-6609 or write TomSuperCoach@gmail.com

or visit www.TomSuperCoach.com

or Tom's blog: www.BeHeardandBeTrusted.com

This book was developed and written with care. Names and details were modified to respect privacy.

Disclaimer: The author and publisher acknowledge that each person's situation is unique, and that readers have full responsibility to seek consultations with health, financial, spiritual and legal professionals. The author and publisher make no representations or warranties of any kind, and the author and publisher shall not be liable for any special, consequential or exemplary damages resulting, in whole or in part, from the reader's use of, or reliance upon, this material.:

Other Books by Tom Marcoux:
- Be Heard and Be Trusted: How to Get What You Want
- Nothing Can Stop You This Year!
- Reduce Clutter, Enlarge Your Life
- Darkest Secrets of Persuasion and Seduction Masters
- Darkest Secrets of Charisma
- Darkest Secrets of Negotiation Masters
- Darkest Secrets of the Film and Television Industry Every Actor Should Know
- Darkest Secrets of Making a Pitch to the Film and Television Industry
- Darkest Secrets of Film Directing
- Truth No One Will Tell You

Praise for *Yes! Secrets for Your Best Life* and Tom Marcoux
• "In *Yes! Secrets for Your Best Life*, Tom Marcoux shares the truth about how you can create success and happiness through the Law of Attraction *plus* the Law of Creation and the Law of Being. These insights will help you step up your game and enjoy each day. Get this book!"
– Dr. JoAnn Dahlkoetter, author of *Your Performing Edge* and coach to CEOs and Olympic Gold Medalists
• "You'll be inspired by Tom Marcoux's sincere efforts to help you resolve problems. I recommend his work to anyone in a pickle."
– David Barron, co-author of *Power Persuasion*

Praise for Tom Marcoux's Other Work:
• "In *Reduce Clutter, Enlarge Your Life*, Marcoux will help you get rid of the physical and mental clutter occupying precious space in your life. You'll reclaim wasted energy, lower your stress, and find time for new opportunities." – Laura Stack, author of *Execution IS the Strategy*
• "In *Power Time Management*, Tom Marcoux shares his extraordinary strategies and methods that save you time, make you money and increase your success and happiness. As Tom's client for many years, I have benefited from his wisdom and strategic approach. Do your career and personal life a big favor and get this book." – Dr. JoAnn Dahlkoetter, author of *Your Performing Edge* and to CEOs and Olympic Gold Medalists
• "When you want to get big things done, persuasion skills are crucial. In *Create Your Best Life*, Tom Marcoux shows you how to develop new reflexes and responses so you can become even more influential under stressful situations. As a journalist and publicist, I've observed how some people come across as charismatic and influential, while others fail to get their message across. Tom Marcoux reveals methods that anyone can use to enhance their charisma and influence—and make a big, positive difference in this world ne!" – Danek S. Kaus, author of *You Can Be Famous: Insider Secrets to Getting Free Publicity*
• "In *Darkest Secrets of Persuasion and Seduction Masters*, learn useful countermeasures to protect you from being darkly manipulated."
– David Barron, co-author, *Power Persuasion*
• "In *Be Heard and Be Trusted*, Tom's advice on how to remain true to yourself and establish authentic rapport with clients is both insightful and reality based. He [shows how] to establish oneself as a credible expert."
-Arthur P. Ciaramicoli, Ed.D., Ph.D., author *The Curse of the Capable*

Visit Tom's blog: www.BeHeardandBeTrusted.com

CONTENTS

Dedication and Acknowledgments	I
Book One: Improve Your Life by Combining the Law of Attraction, Law of Creation and Law of Being	7
Articles are interspersed in this book . . . by guest authors Jeanna Gabellini, Morgana Rae, Rebecca Morgan, Craig Harrison, and Molly Nece	
Law of Creation (3 Steps to Make More Money) . . . More about the Law of Attraction	16
Book Two: The Law of Creation - Wake Up Your Spirit to Prosperity	103
Book Three: The Law of Attraction - Additional Topics	185
Book Four: The Law of Creation - Additional Topics	199
Book Five: The Law of Being - Additional Topics	205
Book Six: Your Springboard to Strength and Success	217
A Final Word and Springboard to Your Success	247
Excerpt from *Darkest Secrets of Persuasion and Seduction Masters: How to Protect Yourself and Turn the Power to Good*	249
About the Author Tom Marcoux	256
Special Offer Just for Readers of this Book	258

DEDICATION AND ACKNOWLEDGEMENTS

This book is dedicated to the terrific book and film consultant, and author Johanna E. Mac Leod. It is also dedicated to the other team members. Thanks to Barry Adamson II and David MacDowell Blue for editing. Thanks to team members who gave comments about the *Wake Up Your Spirit to Prosperity* section of this book: Stacy Diane Horn, Linda Chappo, Dave Strand and my father Al Marcoux.

Thanks to guest authors Molly Nece, Craig Harrison, Jeanna Gabellini, Morgana Rae and Rebecca Morgan. [Their articles remain with their original copyright and are included in this book by their permission.]

Thanks to Judita Bacinskaite for rendering this book's front cover. Thank you Johanna E. Mac Leod for the back cover. Thanks to my father, Al Marcoux, for his concern and efforts for me. Thanks to my mother, Sumiyo Marcoux, a kind, generous soul. Thank you to Higher Power. Thanks to our readers, audiences, clients, my graduate/college students and my team members of
Tom Marcoux Media, LLC. The best to you.

BOOK ONE: IMPROVE YOUR LIFE BY COMBINING THE LAW OF ATTRACTION, LAW OF CREATION AND LAW OF BEING

The airplane wing raced toward my cameraman's head. He was supposed to crouch down and let the wing swoosh safely over him. But he was standing. As the feature film director, I watched the whole set—in this case, the runway at San Luis Obispo airport. I ran, grabbed the cameraman, pulled him downward—and the wing cut the air above our heads.

As I caught my breath, I was grateful that I had not hesitated and that I had acted swiftly to protect my crew member. And I was grateful and excited that *I was directing my first feature film.*

Later, upon reflection, I realized that *manifesting* my big, first-time director opportunity was not just the product of the Law of Attraction. Two other Laws were involved: the *Law of Creation* and the *Law of Being*.

In a moment, I'll provide "working definitions" of the Three Laws: Law of Attraction, Law of Creation and Law of Being.

First, let's observe: **The combined effect of the Three Laws is creating your life of prosperity, love, joy and fulfillment.** For you to experience these benefits, I serve as your coach in this book.

Now, here are the definitions:

Law of Attraction: The operating principle of the universe that "similar energies are drawn together." Positive thoughts act like magnets to positive life experiences and negative thoughts (given too much attention) attract negative life experiences.

Law of Creation: The operating principle of the universe that when you take action you create new possibilities. Often you are creating new impressions in other people's thoughts. People start to view you as a "mover and shaker." Their confidence in you and your project increases. Action breeds more action and more attraction of people and resources to make your dreams come true.

Law of Being: The operating principle of the universe that renewal and gratitude nourish you so you can have sustained prosperity, abundance and fulfillment. The central idea of the Law of Being is to shift to an empowered state of being. A reliable way to experience more joy and peace is to focus on what you're grateful for.

* * *

With this section, I want us to hit the ground running. So I'll now provide brief and pertinent information about *the Three Laws*.

When I reflected on the successes that my clients and I have enjoyed in life, I realized that *the combined effect of the Three Laws* manifests amazing, positive outcomes.

I then taught this to my clients, audiences and students in a quick memorable form: **the 3 A's.**

The 3 A's:
- Attraction
- Action
- Abundance

We can see how the elements correspond:
- Attraction (Law of Attraction)
- Action (Law of Creation)
- Abundance (Law of Being).

Now we'll explore further . . .

Law of Attraction

I'll now focus on two elements of the Law of Attraction:

1) To really invoke the Law of Attraction, go beyond the standard "Ask, Believe, Receive" process.
2) The Law of Attraction involves both spiritual and physical processes.

1) To really invoke the Law of Attraction, go beyond the standard "Ask, Believe, Receive" process.

A truly popular description of the Law of Attraction process is: "Ask, Believe, Receive." You get clear about a personal heartfelt desire; then you ask the universe for that desire. Then you visualize the actual experience of receiving the desired outcome or object. Such visualization involves as many senses as possible. You come to truly *believe* that the desired outcome is yours. And the universe delivers what you want.

I've learned that the Law of Attraction process has many layers and textures.

What really helps is to create *a combined effect* of the three laws: Law of Attraction, Law of Creation and Law of Being.

What's missing from many people's attempt to use the Law of Attraction is *action*. Take action (invoke the Law of Creation) and discover that you become even more attractive to positive outcomes, opportunities and resources.

2) The Law of Attraction involves both spiritual and physical processes.

Numerous people report that their prayers attracted good outcomes. Others suggest that after coming to peace about a situation through meditating, they enjoyed a positive resolution to a conflict-laden situation.

By these examples, it's easy to see a spiritual connection with the Law of Attraction.

The law of attraction is the attractive, magnetic power of the Universe that draws similar energies together. It manifests through the power of creation, everywhere and in multiple ways. . . . This law attracts thoughts, ideas, people, situations and circumstances. The law of attraction manifests through your thoughts, by drawing to you thoughts and ideas of a similar kind, people who think like you, and also corresponding situations and circumstances. It is the law and power that brings together people of similar interests. - Remez Sasson

Further, some people suggest that the Law of

Attraction may be describing part of the effect of mirror neurons. Mirror neurons are brain cells in the premotor cortex that respond when we perform an action and also when we see someone else perform that action. (noted at The DNA Learning Center website). Research has demonstrated that when people view altruistic or positive behaviors by other people, the same neurons are stimulated in the observers' brains.

You can note this for yourself. Recall a time that you approached someone in a positive manner and the person responded in kind with positive cooperation. In essence, your brain cells stimulated the other person's brain cells to a good outcome.

Now It's Your Turn

Verify the efficacy of the Law of Attraction. Can you recall a time when you thought of a friend, and he or she immediately called you on the phone? Do you remember holding a positive expectation and then you walked into a situation and people cooperated well? Some people report that they told themselves, "I'm going to impress them during the job interview"—and in turn, the job interview went extremely well!

Law of Creation

Two elements of the Law of Creation are:
1) The Law of Creation *enhances* the Law of Attraction.
2) The Law of Creation functions at its peak when you invoke the spiritual processes of nonjudgment, nonresistance and nonattachment.

1) The Law of Creation *enhances* the Law of Attraction.

Several people have complained bitterly that they have

practiced "Ask, Believe, Receive" but no heartfelt, desired outcome manifested.

On the other hand, successful people report that they have taken massive amounts of action. They report that such activity made the real difference.

Why would this be so? When you do something, you are creating new possibilities. When you take positive action, you increase the energy that guides a positive return on your invested time, effort and attention.

2) The Law of Creation functions at its peak when you invoke the spiritual processes of nonjudgment, nonresistance and nonattachment.

In a few pages below, I present three separate sections that explore nonjudgment, nonresistance and nonattachment in the context of how you can bring more money into your life. Here I will share that nonjudgment, nonresistance and nonattachment *dissolve hesitation and procrastination to your taking action.*

Now It's Your Turn

Verify the efficacy of the Law of Creation. Can you recall a time when you took action and then enjoyed a positive outcome? Perhaps, you sent out a resume and landed a job opportunity just in time.

Law of Being

The Law of Being includes two particular elements:
1) Feeling grateful places you into an empowered state of being.
2) Doing your duty without renewal gums up the system of positive manifesting.

1) Feeling grateful places you into an empowered state of being.

To invoke the Law of Being does not require a weekend away at a spa (although that would be nice!)

It involves consciously changing the direction of your thoughts *to gratitude.*

Remember, if you are criticizing, you are not being grateful. If you are blaming, you are not being grateful. If you are complaining, you are not being grateful. - Rhonda Byrne

A grateful heart supercharges the Law of Attraction and Law of Creation. A grateful heart attracts blessings. If you catch yourself complaining about something in your life, try this method: Quickly say out loud, this phrase (and fill in the blank): "I am grateful for _____."

Here's how it works:

- Oh! They're changing the rules again. They've doubled my work but not my pay. *I am grateful for* steady work.
- Again! My husband left the toilet seat up! *I am grateful that* he really is considerate about 98% of the time. He must be tired.
- Damn! I gained two pounds. *I'm grateful that* I got the new treadmill working and I find it's okay to use when I read and walk simultaneously. Two pounds is better than four. Let's see how I'm doing after four days of 30 minutes on the treadmill daily.

When you focus on gratitude, you have an actual experience of the Abundance already present in your life. (Recall, Abundance is the third part of the 3 A's.)

I've learned that to attract more of what you want, it truly helps to pay attention to blessings you already have.

The universe responds positively. For example, if you take good care of your current finances, often the universe will give you more finances to work with.

I believe if you keep your faith, you keep your trust, you keep the right attitude, if you're grateful, you'll see God open up new doors. - Joel Osteen

The Law of Being flows in your life when you make time and turn your attention to what you are grateful for in this present moment.

A grateful heart is a beginning of greatness. It is an expression of humility. It is a foundation for the development of such virtues as prayer, faith, courage, contentment, happiness, love, and well-being. - James E. Faust

I feel grateful because I have a lot of love in my life.
- Gisele Bundchen

2) Doing your duty without renewal gums up the system of positive manifesting.
Making consistent choices to renew your personal energy forms a vital element of the Law of Being.

This became all too clear to me several years ago. My father repeated a summary of his philosophy when he said, "Do your duty."

"I do my duty and it doesn't make me happy," I replied. From that moment forward, I realized that I needed more than action and attraction. I needed to feel calm, peace and gratitude for the abundance already present in my life.

Related to the Law of Being, I learned about the value

of "just being" after accomplishing a number of things. Mere accomplishments do not add up to happiness. Accomplishments are just *part* of the journey.

I'm grateful for life. And I live it—I believe life loves the liver of it. I live it. - Maya Angelou

An Important Point about Balancing Duty with Renewal

Talk with a beleaguered single mother, and you'll hear how extremely tough it is to take care of one or more children and work, too.

With so much responsibility, she may forego sleep.

Earlier I said, *making consistent choices to renew your personal energy forms a vital element of the Law of Being.*

Here's a real insight: Renewing your personal energy simply makes things function better.

For example, like other entrepreneurs, I awaken in the morning with my mind full of ideas to implement. I'm excited about what I do and I may be tempted to rise without getting enough sleep. However, I'm aware of the Law of Being. So I keep a log of my sleep hours. In this way, I'm making good choices like going back to bed in the morning to get enough sleep.

The Law of Being calls each of us to consciously and consistently make choices that renew our personal energy and feelings of inner peace and joy.

The Law of Being calls on us to devote time and space to rest, renewal and recovery. When you're in a moment of rest, you can realize that you are experiencing a *moment of abundance*. For example, if you rest in a recliner, you have the abundance of that chair in your home. If you eat a good meal to renew your personal energy, you're enjoying the abundance of that meal.

Get the Law of Attraction and the Law of Creation to truly enhance your life: Take action for renewal so the Law of Being works to empower you.

Now It's Your Turn
Verify the efficacy of the Law of Being. Can you recall a time when you got more sleep, felt better and your next day flowed smoothly? Do you agree that renewing your personal energy increases you ability to perform and even attract positive responses in other people?

* * *

We'll now turn our focus on the Law of Creation and the three steps to increase income.

LAW OF CREATION
(3 STEPS)

Law of Creation—Make More Money (Step 1: Nonjudgment)

Have you ever had an idea but immediately thought "That won't work" or "I don't have the skills or education to make that happen"?

Those were instant judgments that likely shut you down.

Worse yet, those may simply have been "voices from your past," perhaps, from a parent or guardian that do NOT apply to you now!

A big problem human beings face is a tendency to

instantly judge things. If you think about it, our ancestors survived because they instantly judged things—like "That animal may kill me so I'll climb this tree!"

Those kind of instant judgments help on the savanna, or if you're in a crosswalk and have to dodge an errant car. But such automatic judgments can paralyze a person on the path to creating wealth.

The truth is: To create wealth you need to do new things. You cannot let instant judgments dissolve your resolve to take action.

In various sections of this book, I emphasize **The Power of Your Second Thought.**

Your first thought may be a judgmental thought that is tied with fear. Your Power manifests in your Second Thought.

It's crucial to condition ourselves to have an *Empowering Second Thought.*

Let's say you have a thought for a new product.

Instant Judgmental Thought: That won't work.

Empowered Second Thought: **What if it could work?** What knowledge, resources or new action may be involved?

The people who get "average results" or "normal results" allow themselves to react to new ideas with *instant judgments*—and only instant judgments.

However, the successful people I've interviewed demonstrated that they could hold a vision and look for ways to make something work.

Here are some Empowered Second Thoughts:
- How can I learn something new to make this work?
- Who can help me?
- Is my heart being called into the new venture?

- Am I just fearful? Or perhaps, I'm a bit excited about new possibilities.

To make more money, many of us will really unleash both the Law of Creation and the Law of Attraction by *practicing nonjudgment*. Instead of staying stuck in instant judgmental thoughts, we stay flexible and ask questions and open the door for further possibilities.

You never suffer from a money problem, you always suffer from an idea problem. – Robert H. Schuller

Now that notion might seem extreme. But Pastor Robert Schuller actually applied the concept of "idea problem" when he wanted to raise millions of dollars to make a Crystal Cathedral.

He gave himself access to a lot of ideas.

To raise $10 million, he wrote:

Find:

1,000 people to donate $1000.

100 people to donate $10,000.

10 people to donate $1 million.

He also asked a prosperous friend about how to raise money. His friend said, "If you were going to hunt moose, you would go where the moose are."

So Robert Schuller took these ideas and found where prosperous people were and began raising the funds. From 1981 to 2010, the Crystal Cathedral served millions who visited (and saw the related, weekly television program "Hour of Power").

I've attended service at the Crystal Cathedral. It's amazing.

And in 2016, after renovations, it will reopen and serve many more.

Get the Law of Creation flowing in your life. Seek to be

nonjudgmental. Be flexible and grow into the next, great chapter of your life.

Principle
Move beyond instant judgmental thoughts. Stay flexible and ask good questions.

Power Questions
How can you stay conscious of your judgmental thoughts? How will you stay flexible and find new resources and new ideas?

Law of Creation—Make More Money (Step 2: Nonresistance)

Would you like prosperity to flow into your life with a minimum of effort and difficulty?

The spiritual practice of *nonresistance* plus the Law of Creation maximizes abundance on many occasions.

For example, when I come up with a book project, I go with my intuition and get right to work. However, there are times when the marketplace will surprise me.

For example, I wrote a book that is another part of my series *Darkest Secrets of... How to Protect Yourself*. The title of this book was *Darkest Secrets of Business Communication*. It discussed ways to help the reader avoid mistakes that often create needless confusion and trouble in the business arena.

However, I was greatly surprised when the book didn't sell many copies. My previous titles including *Darkest Secrets of Persuasion and Seduction Masters* and *Darkest Secrets of Film Directing* had sold copies every month.

I decided to practice *nonresistance*. I came up with a way to greatly revise the material and release it as a 2nd edition entitled: *Secrets of Awesome Dinner Guests: What Walt Disney, Steve Jobs, Oprah Winfrey, Albert Einstein, Martin Luther King, Jr., Helen Keller and John Lasseter Can Teach You About Success and Fulfillment.* Now, the book sells well.

Nonresistance has a *great benefit* to bestow upon you: you avoid needless emotional upset and loss of time.

Here's the big difference. People who get "average results" or "normal results" often resist what the world or reality is telling them.

When my book wasn't selling, the marketplace was telling me: "You're not serving us in the way we want to be served."

I did not waste a moment trying to "educate people." Instead, I found another way that was "enticing to people."

In fact, I relaxed and did a few other things. I did a video that I posted on YouTube entitled "Use Walt Disney's Strategy for Success . . . with Tom Marcoux." The good responses that people posted to me on Facebook inspired me to expand the idea to "Secrets of Awesome Dinner Guests: What Walt Disney . . ." as you saw above.

Practice nonresistance and let the ideas flow.

Principle

Approach a problem in the spirit of flowing and adapting.

Power Questions

How can you adapt to a situation? Can you revise your approach? Can you ask people for ideas about what's really important to them? How can you serve people in the way they prefer to be served?

Law of Creation — Make More Money (Step 3: Nonattachment)

Have you found yourself ruminating about something that is just not going your way? Nonattachment provides a graceful way for you to feel better and even get more done.

The essence of nonattachment is to turn "demands" into "preferences."

For example, if Shirley insists that the only good result is for her first book to be a bestseller, then she may face huge disappointment. The result of "bestseller" is only *one* of many positive results.

Bestselling author Richard Carlson told me that his top-selling book *Don't Sweat the Small Stuff* was his 10th book. He loved to write and he pressed on through nine books before he had his first bestselling book.

Nonattachment can seem foreign to many people. Certainly we do feel attached to our friends and family. However, we can enjoy better relationships with them if we do NOT insist that they act, always in the way we think best.

As a comparative religion instructor guiding college students for over 12 years, I have explained, "Nonattachment is having preferences and NOT demands."

When you walk into situations without a demand, you can "be in this present moment."

One does not stay in the past with regrets or anger

about a family member's unkind remarks, for example. And one does not "go into the future"—worrying about poor treatment.

For example, my father is in his late 70s and his comments (as he gets older) have been mean to family members. He is an upset, unhappy, old guy.

When I travel to visit my father and mother, I have no idea what will happen, that is, whether my father will be mean or neutral with his words.

I seek to "walk into the moment fresh." Here's one reason: To walk into the moment already upset over past bad behavior by my father does *not* help.

A number of spiritual paths urge people to not attach themselves to an idea of how they want someone else to be. People only change when they want to.

Otherwise, the person who demands another person be different creates his or her *own* internal suffering.

Before we go further, it would help for me to clarify that there can be "non-negotiables"—particularly in romantic relationships. For example, one of my clients told her boyfriend, "No illegal drugs in my home. I am a school teacher." It's perfectly understandable that she wants to guard her reputation and that she is attached to her job teaching grammar kids. That's a straight forward non-negotiable detail.

However, if we hold to the idea of nonattachment, we can actually feel inner peace and enjoy the moments as they arrive.

Here's how we can be non-attached when we're looking to create more prosperity.

Gently ask questions like:
- Will this serve many people?
- Does this have a good chance to make profit?

- Will we learn something by doing it?

Some projects are "the projects that train us to do better next time."

For example, actress and singer Cher, starred in the 1969 feature film *Chastity*. The film flopped badly, and it's reported Cher avoided acting for more than a decade due to the debacle.

Anyone who saw *Chastity* would *not* imagine that Cher would win the Best Actress Academy Award in 1988 for *Moonstruck*.

Good for Cher! She took courageous steps forward.

At some point, *many people find it necessary to shake off the dust of defeat and move forward.*

Nonattachment comes in when we focus on doing our best *in this moment*.

You learn that the fulfilling part is the doing.

– Ed Harris (nominated for 4 Academy Awards)

Ed refers to acting, and he mentioned that one of his own favorite performances is in the feature film *Copying Beethoven*. He was pained that the distributor did not promote the film on release.

So Ed's full comment is: "You learn that the fulfilling part is the doing. I don't count on anything else."

My point about nonattachment is that as you stay flexible you'll be able to leap at new opportunities that will surprise you. It's said that comedian Jimmy Durante began more as a musician. But he saw how people related to his big nose and jokes and threw himself into comedy. Such a move led to his stardom.

Truly, when you want to create more prosperity in your life, use the wisdom and the peace of nonattachment.

Principle
Free up your possibilities. Move beyond staying attached to first judgments or even disappointments. Be flexible.

Power Questions
How can you reframe your perception on some disappointments? Could they be a springboard to your next chapter of life?

Law of Attraction and Clearing the Blocks

A number of people report that they attempt to use the classic three steps of the Law of Attraction: Ask, Believe, Receive but they do *not* get the results they crave.

What's going on here? Some of us have strong, subconscious blocks that interfere with the Law of Attraction fully working in our lives.

Here are examples of Blocks:
A person . . .
- feels twisted about money
- feels unworthy of success
- feels his or her success "takes away" from someone else
- feels afraid of losses that may come with success
- does not feel a Deep Need to do what's necessary to succeed

To get the Law of Attraction working well, turn these around:
A person
- feels clean and comfortable about money
- feels worthy and happy about success

- feels his or her personal success serves other people
- feels strong and able to withstand the losses that may come with success—and feels sure that the losses "make space" for better people, things and opportunities to now fit into one's life
- feels (everyday) a Deep Need to do what's necessary to succeed

Clear the Blocks

Before we get started with clearing the blocks that occur when applying the Law of Attraction, realize that these blocks begin on the subconscious level. So I'm including sections labeled "Working on the Subconscious Level" in the material below.

1. Clear a feeling of "twisted about money"

Years ago, I had a roommate who was comfortable about money. If he saw that the household box was low on funds, he'd simply go to the roommates and say, "Oh, the household box is a bit low. We're saving to paint the kitchen. Would you get in your monthly contribution before Thursday?"

This roommate even ran a church in which he posted the church's full budget of income and expenditures in the newsletter. My roommate was "clean and comfortable about money." You could even see his exact salary, which was low.

He did not let himself sit in embarrassment about his low salary.

I'm *not* inviting you to reveal your salary to other people. However, I am inviting you to "reveal your money situation to *yourself*." By this I mean, ask yourself, "Do I have limiting beliefs about money that are holding me back?"

A number of authors point out that limiting beliefs can *restrict* our actions. A limiting belief is recognized by how it stops you from entertaining the possibility of making a true, positive change. It might be characterized by the whining phrase: "It will never work." Limiting beliefs prevent us from making empowering choices.

Worse yet, if you act in a self-sabotaging manner you could be shutting down the efficacy of the Law of Attraction in your life! Further, failing to act can also be self-sabotage.

The following limiting beliefs contribute to what I call "twisted about money."

- Money is the root of all evil. [The actual Biblical quote is: "The *love* of money is the root of all evil."]
- You have to give up too much to be wealthy.
- "Behind every great fortune lies a great crime." – Honore de Balzac

That last comment about "great crime" is one that my father has repeated many times, and I witnessed how he could *not* bring himself to save any money. This limiting belief also *prevented* my father from looking at multiple ways to earn money.

To stop my father's "great crime" comment from being a virus to hurt me, I immediately remind myself of the *benevolent prosperity* author Richard Carlson earned. I've coined the term "benevolent prosperity" to refer to a fortune built on truly serving others. Richard served others as author and speaker. He was best known for writing the *Don't Sweat the Small Stuff* series of books. I know he earned $20,000 a speech (a high fee several years ago) because one of my colleagues called to hire him for her conference.

When Richard Carlson and I were both guest experts on a radio show, he went out of his way to share with me tips for enhancing my work as a speaker and author. What a good and kind mentor!

Richard Carlson is one of the shining examples that *you can add good work to the world and the world provides abundance right back.*

Here's a phrase I tell myself: *Money is a tool I handle well for my good and all involved.*

When I affirm that phrase, I repeatedly remind myself that my earning money ultimately serves all involved. It is a good thing.

Working on the Subconscious Level

I've learned that impacting the subconscious mind takes multiple approaches.

One powerful approach is to *consciously monitor your stories:* stories you tell others, stories you watch and listen to, and *stories you tell yourself.*

Stories are what stick with you.

So our first method is: **Replace the Stuck Story**. I describe the Stuck Story as any tale that holds you back.

Consider telling yourself stories that involve positive outcomes. Make it a conscious choice. It can be a simple story of "I found $5.00 on the bus. I'm lucky."

Also tell stories about how other people performed good deeds, earned opportunities and became prosperous.

2. Clear the feeling of "unworthy of success"

Years ago, I was in Hollywood, running an audition. As both writer and feature film director, I was looking for a rising actor to play the lead ("Alan") of a screenplay I wrote titled, *TimePulse**. I also put out the word that we were looking for the two women leads as well.

I had five people sort through 807 submitted headshots (photos of actors). I saw 21 people in one day.

The big test (although the actors auditioning for "Alan" did not know it) was how the actors would say a particular line.

"Sir Gawain was being tested to see if he was worthy or not."

I was hoping to see the actors study the pages and find the hidden key to the scene. When Alan tells the story and says "worthy or not" he's talking about *himself*.

That day, no actor found a way to communicate the line in a way that showed me he had *become* the lead character. The character Alan is a guy who talks about stories of "feeling unworthy." He *does not* feel worthy.

Feeling worthy or not is *big deal* when it comes to the Law of Attraction and receiving the abundance of the universe.

If you practice telling the story that you are not worthy enough or good enough, *the universe will take you at your word*. This can be terrible. It even becomes a self-fulfilling prophesy. A person can accumulate experiences in which something good was about to happen but then "things fell apart." If someone adds, "Oh, I wasn't ready, anyway," it can add more injury. It can block off the Law of Attraction in helping you through life.

What's the answer?: **Stop telling those "unworthy me" stories! I mean it.**

There are some confusing details that trip many people up. We see confusion among these words: Proud, Stuck up, Conceited, Self-Esteem, Arrogant, Self-centered.

* TimePulse *became a book:* TimePulse Beyond: Titanic *available at* Amazon.com

Self-esteem is NOT connected to the other words. Here is a valuable definition:

"Self-esteem is the disposition to experience oneself as being competent to cope with the basic challenges of life and of being worthy of happiness. It is confidence in the efficacy of our mind, in our ability to think. By extension, it is confidence in our ability to learn, make appropriate choices and decisions, and respond effectively to change. It is also the experience that success, achievement, fulfillment—happiness—are right and natural for us. The survival-value of such confidence is obvious; so is the danger when it is missing." – Nathaniel Branden

In a nutshell, self-esteem is *not* about self-centeredness. Instead, self-esteem is about having the capacity to cope with challenges in life and the ability to thrive!

Further, not having self-esteem, or feeling unworthy, can create a terrible block to a good flow of the Law of Attraction.

There is a controversy about the ways to raise self-esteem. A number of people report that using affirmations like "I feel terrific" actually make them feel worse. They report, "I do not like lying to myself. It feels even worse."

So now, we'll turn our attention to a powerful idea:

It's easier to act your way into a new way of thinking, than think your way into a new way of acting. – Jerry Sternin*

[* There are numerous people who reference this idea. It's not clear who said it first.]

So instead of just repeating certain phrases, I invite you to *take action.* Below, I share the method: **Prove It to Yourself.**

Working on the Subconscious Level
Our second method is: **Prove It to Yourself.** Start proving

it to yourself that you are worthy of success. How? Be good to other people. Watch yourself being good to other people. Do helpful actions whether it's simply opening a door for someone or helping a child with homework.

If you're selling something, make sure that the person has a good buying experience. After a week, I'm still telling people about my good experience created by an expert salesman who sold me my recent suits.

Tell stories about how you're helping people. When you talk about how you've helped someone, you're programming yourself on the subconscious level that you ARE a good person doing good!

3. Clear the feeling that one's success "takes away" from someone else

Have you met some people who seemed to be stuck in "scarcity thinking"? From the way they talk, it seems they are trying to push the *supposition* that anyone's good fortune takes away from others.

However, when people actually take time to study the efforts of a number entrepreneurs, they uncover many projects that have *significantly improved the lives of many people!*

For example, Sara Blakely came up with the idea Spanx, known as an undergarment that gives the wearer a slim and shapely appearance.

Based on her ingenuity and efforts, Sara became a billionaire. Did she take away anything? No. She came up with an idea and put people to work, and she gave many women a feeling that they looked better. Spanx became so pervasive that it was featured in the movie *The Heat*. Sandra Bullock's character was wearing Spanx and said, "They're my Spanx. They hold everything together."

Further, Sara established The Sara Blakely Foundation to help women through education and entrepreneurial training. Sara also donated $1 million to the Oprah Winfrey Leadership Academy for Girls in South Africa.

This is just one of many examples with regards to people doing good and reaping the rewards of abundance.

Working on the Subconscious Level

Our third method is: **Replace Inky Water.** The process helps you force out limiting beliefs.

Imagine that you have a bucket of clear water, but you contaminate it with ink, and soon all the water appears black.

One way to clear out the bucket would be to pour in clear water consistently until all the inky water is forced out.

We use this metaphor by identifying the inky water as contaminated thinking made of limiting beliefs. At this moment, we're targeting the limiting belief that "one's success takes away from someone else."

When we examine the Law of Attraction in action, we can find numerous examples of entrepreneurs developing new ideas, new markets, new jobs, and other new opportunities.

This also reminds me of individuals who complain that actor Robert Downey, Jr. did not "deserve" to earn $50 million for his role as Iron Man in *Marvel's The Avengers*, a film that earned $1.5 billion. A journalist calculated that with all the people who saw the film, Robert Downey, Jr. earned $0.25 per person. Considering the entertainment value he brought to the project, is it okay that he earned 25 cents per person?

People on track to receive abundance and welcome opportunities via the Law of Attraction tend to reply, "Yes!"

How much does Robert Downey, Jr. give to charity? Who

knows?

However, it's been reported that Angelina Jolie uses this plan: 1/3 of her income goes to charity, 1/3 goes to savings and 1/3 she lives on with her family.

Many of us would say, "Sounds good."

The method of *Replace Inky Water* is to keep filling your mind with positive examples and thoughts about abundance. Such positive material is clear water replacing inky water, and in turn, abundance thinking replacing scarcity thinking. **In doing so, we notice that there are people who innovate and keep making the "pie" [what's available to people] bigger and bigger.**

In essence, when I'm talking about the strategy Replace Inky Water, I'm inviting you to gather the evidence and convince yourself that more abundance can be made.

Here's another example. Before 1995's *Toy Story*, there had been no feature length computer-animated films.

In 1995, *Toy Story* earned $361.9 million. It opened a new form of entertainment.

In the year, 2012, there were several computer-animated films from various studios:

2012 (computer animated films' earnings):
Brave - $539 million
Wreck-It Ralph - $471.2 million
Hotel Transylvania - $385.3 million
Rise of the Guardians - $306.9 million
Ice Age 4 - $877.2 million
The Lorax - $348.8 million
Madagascar 3 - $746.9 million

The above shows that the "pie" or levels of abundance can expand and expand.

The person who wants the Law of Attraction to flow in his or her life will take the above details and realize they support abundance thinking. You can consistently use abundance thinking to persistently replace the stagnant effects of scarcity thinking.

How will *you* consistently and daily fill your mind with "the clear water of abundance thinking"?

4. Clear the feeling of fear of losses that may come with success

Several years ago, I had a particular close friend "Bob" who dropped a few of his friends. I watched this and a clear *intuitive thought* came to me: "Bob is going to drop me when one of my entrepreneurial projects brings in big income. He'll make up some reason to be mad at me and then he'll disappear from my life."

I expressed my concern to Bob and surprise—he did *not* say, "No, Tom. That won't happen."

A couple of months later, he dropped me even *before* my big project-success.

I really grieved about Bob disappearing from my life: We had been friends for over 21 years. There were many good times, but the friendship was no more.

My point with sharing this story is: I learned something important:

Some friendships are like novels.

Some friendships are like short stories.

And some friendships are a sentence. (Put a period on that thing and end it!)

My point is that when I took a close look at my relationship with Bob, I realized that he, at times, would tear down my entrepreneurial efforts. So ultimately, it was a relief to lose Bob from my life.

I'll put this in a few words: as you become successful, you

will lose a few things—and, most likely, a few friendships.

But being yourself and living on your true path is worth it!

Besides, we all lose things and people on the path.

Just two months ago, a close friend, Harry, died. I lost him. Today, I caught myself automatically dialing his phone number. I stopped dialing.

The week of his death, I called Harry's voicemail system to hear his voice. His outgoing voicemail message sounded like he was bored and tired. That was *not* my friend!

So I let it go. I did *not* record that message. I let go of trying to hold on to some remnant of my dear friend.

You see, we all flow thorough different "chapters" in our lives. It helps to practice letting go.

As you become more and more successful, you enter new chapters in life and some people will not want to go into the new chapter with you.

Consider developing yourself so you feel strong and able to withstand the losses that may come with success—and feel sure that the losses "make space" for better people, things and opportunities to now fit into your life.

I know this can be hard. At times, I still feel sad that a chapter (with my friendship with Bob) *closed* in my life. But here's the crucial detail: Would I go back? No!

The answer to the fear of about success and related losses is to add a new empowering thought—or what I call the **Empowered Link.**

Working on the Subconscious Level

Our fourth method is: **Add Empowered Link.**

A number of long-time practitioners of meditation (such as Buddhist monks) report that they avoid thoughts of suffering. That is, after years and thousands of hours of meditation, they rarely think disquieting thoughts.

Personally, I have NOT meditated enough to avoid having disquieting thoughts. The majority of my clients have not risen to the "monk-level of meditating."

So what do we do with disquieting thoughts?

We can use the method of the *Empowered Link*.

A disquieting thought arises and you *Link* an *Empowering Thought* to it. In essence, you "cancel out" the first thought, which is harmful, and replace it with a thought that is empowering.

Researchers suggest that we have 12,000 to 70,000 thoughts per day. Much of these thoughts are automatic, negative, "re-run" thoughts. They're just conditioned thoughts that pop up whenever a present stimulus is similar to a stimulus from our past.

For example, when I was in 7th grade, I went to a classmate "Susan" and asked, "Can I walk you home?"

She replied with a sneer, "What for?!" In front of her sister. I ran home, lost my keys during that run and got in big trouble. I never found the keys.

It would have been easy to let the disquieting thought: "Beware of all girls with long, brown hair and glasses!" run my life.

Instead, I learned to have the Empowering Thought: *"I'm talking to a new person here. This is a new moment."*

Doing so, empowered me to not shy away from the rejection on might endure in the pursuit of love, and I was *not* prevented from having girlfriends in my later years.

I'm suggesting that *you pay attention* to your disquieting thoughts and make an Empowered Link.

Here's another example: Years ago, any time I would complain about a particular job I did just to earn rent money, I would immediately add this *Empowered Thought:* "I am grateful for steady work."

Immediately, I felt better!

So in this section, we're talking about the disquieting thought: "If I'm successful, I'm going to lose something or someone."

You could develop your own Empowered Link: *"Losses may happen, but that makes space for better opportunities and good people in my life."*

You could use another version: *"I can handle it. More opportunities and people are waiting to greet me!"*

Now it's your turn.

How can you add an *Empowered Link* (or automatic empowered thought) to any recurring fearful thought you may have about becoming successful?

Remember the Empowered Link process is about consciously choosing to add an Empowered Thought to any recurring fearful thought. In this way, you avoid blocking the flow that the Law of Attraction has to offer. You, by your own self-chosen conditioning, place yourself into an empowered state of being.

5. Clear the "hesitation block" and feel (everyday) a Deep Need to do what's necessary to succeed

What is holding many people back from more success? They do *not* feel a Deep Need to do what's necessary to succeed.

This is a profound realization.

We're not goofing around here. We are not talking about having a wish to have a little more money. *We* ***are*** *talking about making big, meaningful improvements in life and happiness!*

In my book, *Reduce Clutter, Enlarge Your Life*, I shared this story:

"My client, Joseph, rented a large storage locker filled with junk—for 20 years. His wife occasionally complained about the expense.

Joseph worked long hours and explained that he did not have the energy or time to devote to reducing the amount of junk in his storage locker.

Then one day, he read a paragraph of a book that showed how one can lose thousands of dollars over a span of years while renting a storage locker. In essence, one pays so much rent that one could buy the objects 20 times over.

I asked Joseph to literally calculate how much money he would save if he reduced the size of his storage locker down to a 4 x 5 locker for only $64.00 per month.

He calculated that he could save $4,944.00 in a couple of years.

Still he was not moved.

Then, Joseph told me that one of his family members expressed her big wish was to go to Walt Disney World in 2017 and see James Cameron's Avatarland (based on the blockbuster feature film *Avatar*).

I invited Joseph to focus on the possibility of making his loved one's dream come true. "Think of how $4,944 will help you make a family trip possible," I said.

Boom! Now, Joseph had a **Huge Reason** to tackle the hassle of getting rid of a bunch of junk.

He immediately took action that day and rented the $64.00 storage locker and moved 5 boxes of "definitely keep" material into the new storage locker."

Upon additional reflection, I realized multiple principles involved in the above story:

Not only did Joseph have a Huge Reason, he also *had a Deep Need to do his best in making life good and happy for his loved one.*

You can read all the books and try different methods for a month or two to increase your income, but you may not make a break through. And that is because you may not possess in your mind a Deep Need to do what is necessary to succeed.

To have the Law of Attraction flow well in your life, you need to AIM IT at something that you feel deeply in your heart!

That's what I'm referring to with the story of Joseph taking massive action to make the dream of his family member come true.

To be rich, you cannot be normal. – Noah St. John

So-called "normal" or "average" people, will simply not do what committed professionals will do.

They won't rehearse for hours; they won't study daily; they won't bear the price of scorn by friends and family.

I'm am not saying that living your best life is easy. I AM saying that it's worth it . . . when you connect with your Deep Need.

For many of us, our Deep Need is to be good to a loved one or perhaps, a cause.

And many of us are similar: We'll do more for someone else than ourselves.

And then, there are entrepreneurs who simply want to see an idea become reality in the world. Steve Jobs said, "I want to put a dent in the universe."

Recently, I read *Think and Grow Rich for Women*, the expanded version of the original book, *Think and Grow Rich* by Napoleon Hill. In her book for women, author Sharon Lechter shared that every day she does 2-2-2 . . . that's two emails, two handwritten notes and two posts in social media. In this way she is always filling "the pipeline"—that is, she is always attracting new business.

I have a question. What Deep Need would move you to adopt a discipline like Sharon's "2-2-2"?

Working on the Subconscious Level

Our fifth method is: **Face the Reality of Your Deep Need.**

One of my Deep Needs has its genesis in my facing tough times immediately upon graduating from college.

I needed to swiftly raise money to fund a feature film that I was going to direct. Back then, we did *not* have Amazon, Wikipedia and other resources. There was no Linkedin, Facebook or Kickstarter to connect with anyone. I wasn't even in Los Angeles. Instead, I was in a little town in Northern California.

I did NOT know what to do. I was terrified and desperate. I had some people with me but everyone turned to me to pull off the miracle of getting strangers to invest in an unknown director (me) and an unknown team. It was one of the lowest points of my life. I retreated. I'd write the screenplay all night long, awaken late in the day, and feel relieved that I didn't have to confront strangers that day. It was already 5 pm so I was "off the hook."*

Even so I was at a complete loss. I was desperate; I didn't know where to turn. So this terribly painful experience inspired one of my Deep Needs . . .

One of my Deep Needs is to be equipped and armed for the tough battles of life.

So everyday, I study—reading books and new articles about various aspects of business, deal-making, team leadership and more.

[*Several years later, I wrote the book that I really needed back when I had just graduated; I titled it: *Darkest Secrets of Making a Pitch for the Film and Television Industry: How You Can Get a Studio Executive, Producer, Name Actor or Private Investor to Say "Yes" to Your Project.*]

I refuse to be caught again (like in my twenties) without a bunch of case histories and principles in my mind so that I will have an edge in whatever next business challenge I face.

Each year, I read around 85 books to keep up and stay prepared.

Now, it's your turn.

What has really hurt you? Where are the sources of your Deep Needs?

Can you use the past pain as *Present Fuel* so you'll do what's necessary to succeed today and tomorrow?

Every top successful person I have interviewed has demonstrated that they are fueled by both positive intentions and also Deep Needs to overcome past pain.

I always remember one particular case history I read more than ten years ago.

Back in the 50's, a new bride went to her husband and asked for $10.00.

"What for?" her husband demanded.

"Nothing," she said, offended. From that moment forward, she resolved to never ask him for money again.

She got a job and then started her own business and became prosperous with her own efforts. Good for her!

And, we can see that her success was in part fueled by her past pain and her Deep Need to be independent and never humiliated about money again!

Now, let's shift gears. A Deep Need may be fueled by a positive intention. For example, as I mentioned earlier, a number of us will do more for someone we love than for ourselves. You can use that as your Deep Need to do what's necessary to succeed.

Pull out a sheet of paper or type into a laptop, *what deeply moves you to action.*

The sooner you get clear on this, the more powerful you become in using it and the faster you get at moving forward.

I call the above details the process of *Face the Reality of Your Deep Need*. For many of us, the underlying cause for us to get into action may *not* be something we want to discuss at the dinner table.

Use the truth about yourself to take action and open the door for the Law of Attraction to *really* work in your life.

* * *

In summary, here are the methods to help you remove the blocks so the Law of Attraction functions well in your life:

1. Replace the Stuck Story
2. Prove It to Yourself
3. Replace Inky Water
4. Add the Empowered Link
5. Face the Reality of Your Deep Need

Principle

Free up your possibilities. Replace limiting beliefs with the true power of your Deep Need. Use discipline to get your brain to serve you in better ways.

Power Questions

What personal stories (and case histories) inspire you?

How can you prove it to yourself that your success is already helping others?

What limiting beliefs do you want to crowd out of your mind?

What Empowered Thought do you want linked to a recurring fearful thought you have?

How can you use your Deep Need to get you into consistent action?

Enjoy Enhancing Your Courage through the Law of Attraction

Imagine feeling great courage. The Law of Attraction can help you with this. For some of us, the idea of the Law of Attraction is comforting. It can be understood by thinking: "If I think positively, then positive outcomes are surely on their way to me."

The law of attraction is the attractive, magnetic power of the Universe that draws similar energies together. It manifests through the power of creation, everywhere and in multiple ways. – Remez Sasson

So the idea that the Universe will get behind you and help you manifest what you truly want can enhance your courage.

On the other hand, some people feel fear related to the ideas of the Law of Attraction. They might have certain thoughts enter their mind like this: "Wait a minute! If I'm worried about something, I will draw exactly what I fear to me!"

I've learned that while fearful thoughts do occur, the answer is to condition yourself to think empowering thoughts after a fearful thought. I call this **The Power of Your Second Thought.**

To manifest what you really want often requires courage.

I learned that courage was not the absence of fear, but the triumph over it. *The brave man is not he who does not feel afraid, but he who conquers that fear. – Nelson Mandela*

Here's where courage comes in. Some people think of a big, positive dream for their lives but then feel fear. "What if it doesn't work out? What if I lose money? What if I look foolish and my friends and family make fun of me?"

It takes a great deal of bravery to stand up to our enemies, but just as much to stand up to our friends. – J. K. Rowling

The courage part is to keep moving forward in spite of the fear.

To use the Law of Attraction in your favor, do take time and think of what you really want. Then do not just stay in that one mode of thinking. Start getting more information and training—and Take Action!

Now I'm going to share really practical methods. Knowing and using these practical methods will build up your positive thoughts (attracting positive outcomes).

We'll use the C.A.N. process:

C – cover the downside

A – arrange your own approval

N – nurture yourself

1. Cover the downside

Inaction breeds doubt and fear. Action breeds confidence and courage. If you want to conquer fear, do not sit home and think about it. Go out and get busy. – Dale Carnegie

Here's an important part of "getting busy."

Make a thorough plan that includes backup details to ensure your continued well-being even if something goes wrong.

Do not shy away from taking action just because you might have to face a disappointing outcome. If I do 20 projects, some of them will not yield the income that I prefer. But I move ahead anyway. How can I do that? Each project has a budget so I can withstand a loss or two because the budget was not too big to "sink the whole company."

That's what I mean by "cover the downside": The downside would be investing money in a project and then that project does not breakeven. To cover the downside would be to strategically keep the budget low.

In essence, that's making a thorough plan that includes allowances for missteps. Having a thorough plan can boost your courage.

Successful people know and use 'the numbers.'

Another way to boost your courage is to "know the important numbers." By this I mean: identify what specific steps and items you need to improve.

Measurement is the first step that leads to control and eventually to improvement. If you can't measure something, you can't understand it. If you can't understand it, you can't control it. If you can't control it, you can't improve it.

– H. James Harrington

Successful people know how much income must be brought in by sales to breakeven and to go into profit.

They know, on average, how many marketing phone calls lead to gaining a new client.

Here's where you boost your courage. If you don't measure things, you will likely have "free floating anxiety" because so many things will be uncertain.

On the other hand, as soon as you write a plan on paper and take some action, you'll feel stronger. Your courage will expand.

Such good thoughts and good feelings, by the Law of Attraction, will bring you better and better results.

2. Arrange your own approval

Let's return to this quote: *It takes a great deal of bravery to stand up to our enemies, but just as much to stand up to our friends. – J. K. Rowling*

I have had friends who could NOT see my vision for projects. They warned me against moving forward. If I had listened to them, I would have been stopped in my tracks. Some projects like my book *Darkest Secrets of Persuasion and Seduction Masters: How to Protect Yourself and Turn the Power to Good* have yielded income every month. So those particular friends were *wrong!*

What happened then? They merely shrugged and said something like: "Oh, well. Some things turn out okay."

Okay! They almost led me down the path of doing nothing and helping nobody. That's serious.

So I invite you to avoid living for anyone else's approval. **Set your own internal and personal standards.** In essence, "arrange your own approval."

3. Nurture yourself

Acting in a courageous manner takes energy and internal reserves. How do you have such reserves? You nurture yourself. I've said to clients: *Take breaks or be broken.*

When you nurture yourself, you build up your resilience. To manifest your dreams you need a big helping of resilience! When you stretch and grow, you'll have some projects and some experiences that really disappoint you. But you can be proud of yourself that you demonstrated courage. You took an appropriate risk. Good for you!

To really get the Law of Attraction working for you, approach your activities with strategy. Use strategy in how you think (habitually) and how you make plans and take action.

Your courage will expand and the Law of Attraction will assist you in manifesting terrific outcomes.

Principle
Enhance the Law of Attraction working *for* you by taking courageous action.

Power Question
How can you nurture yourself so you have the energy to take courageous action?

* * *

Now that I've talked about fear and conditioning yourself to use *the Power of Your Second Thought,* here are insights about fear from Molly Nece.

Face *Your* Fears
by Molly Nece

Everyone has a fear of something. Fear of public speaking, dying, spiders, you name it—everyone has something. Mine was letting go of money in order to gain something more than money could ever buy—a deeper sense of peace and purpose. I had created a very fulfilling career, lived in a loving community, have a loving husband, and a brilliant, kind-hearted child. Why would I need anything more? I felt something was missing, but if only I knew the root cause? I always wanted to pursue my motivational speaking career fulltime, but knew I would miss the team office environment and the consistent bi-weekly paycheck.

Was I ready to take the leap? I didn't believe with my

whole heart that I was ready so I didn't. Instead I knew I had to take steps to face my scarcity mindset of not having enough money. I asked my husband if we could move to a cash budget and see what it would feel like to live on a particular salary. We failed miserably each month in staying within the budget. On the positive side, each month we became more mindful of how we spent our money and where our money was going. After five months of failed attempts to live exactly within the limited budget I set for our family, I realized that it was because we didn't have a shared sense of urgency.

It also gave me the opportunity to keep questioning and seeking deeper meaning behind what I was trying to accomplish. Did I want to leave higher education or simply need a new experience? The answer came clear. I not only wanted a new experience, I wanted to live in a new location—the beach! Luckily, so did my husband and son. As a result, I decided to write the gentleman in a desirable position at a university by the beach. I shared with him that I wanted to move to the area within the next five years and shared my expertise and how I might be able to help him. While I never heard back from him, I didn't give up hope. I continued to explore my options that would fit my passions. Four months later his position was posted, I interviewed, and six months later I was sitting in his chair, developing this most comprehensive training, coaching, and consulting model for faculty and staff the university had ever seen.

While our family initially took a 75% pay cut for the first four months, we discovered that living mindfully financially prior to taking the leap of faith was the best thing we could have ever done. We were also shown that anything is possible when you put passion behind every thought, word, and action. Fear is able to be conquered when one fully believes in the Law of Attraction and the fact that everything you want, wants you. Live fearlessly!

Molly Nece has spent over fifteen years in corporate and higher education administration. Ten of those years have been focused in the field of training and organizational development. Over the past five years, she has enjoyed building two training companies and writing six books. Molly has received her Master's in Training and Organizational Development from West Chester University; Bachelor's degrees in Psychology and Elementary Education from Gettysburg College; and two certificates—Lean Six Sigma from Villanova and Mediation from Lakewood College.

Her vast knowledge is supported with real-life stories and hands on activities that help to motivate her audiences to take action. As a result of her experiences in leadership, service, team strengthening, and productivity, she has gained valuable insight that equips her clients to succeed in both good and challenging economies. Because of these vast and varied experiences, she enjoys helping private, public, non-profit, and religious groups create goldmines both at work and home through The Nece Group. To learn more about how she can help inspire and equip you and your teams to peak performance, go to www.TheNeceGroup.com.

Raise Your Confidence through the Law of Attraction

Want to feel really confident? You *can!* Use the Law of Attraction to do just that. How? I'll illustrate this with a story.

Some years ago, I was casting a feature film. I was directing test footage with a young woman "Ginny" who was auditioning. Ginny turned and her shimmering blond hair flowed. She moved with grace—born of her years as both gymnast and dancer.

In the scene, I was acting, portraying the hero who had no idea that this young woman was from the future. (This was a scene from a screenplay, later a book, I wrote entitled *TimePulse**.

When the camera rolls, any actor can have a degree of fear.

But as a *trained* actor I had an advantage. I was trained to use "the objective." Often as a director, I have asked an actor, "In this moment, what do you want?" The answer "I want____" is the objective.

One of the tough things for an actor to do convincingly is to listen in a scene. If the actor effectively uses *the objective*, he can be real. How? In any moment—in real life—we want something.

So using my objective, I was confident in the scene. I acted *without* novice-actor nervousness.

In the scene, I was completely connected to what the character wants moment to moment.

The videotaped audition went well, and I was clear about what I wanted both as director and producer.

Such confidence was attractive.

In real life, Ginny soon became my girlfriend.

So let's discuss the essence of confidence as expressed in the above story.

Clarity and connection to what you really want often comes across as confidence.

Frankly, it's a real cliché about good directors: "Yes, she really knew what she wanted."

* *TimePulse: Beyond Titanic* has a free chapters at Amazon.com

Here's where the Law of Attraction and confidence mix together.

The Law of Attraction often waits for you to express clarity about what you want. No hesitation. No shyness. Ask for what you want. Focus on what you want.

And if appropriate keep these thoughts to yourself.

Especially do *not* mention your big dreams to pessimists who cannot even imagine that big dreams come true. Such pessimists look upon the achievers of the world as "freaks of nature" or "merely lucky freaks."

The basic form of using the Law of Attraction is *Ask, Believe Receive*. And I celebrate the "ask" part. It's like using *the objective* which is found by answering the question: "What do you want?"

But it's not merely a quiet "What do you want?"

No! It's a loud, powerful *"What do you REALLY want?"*

That's when you engage the Law of Attraction. You proclaim to yourself (and in your mind, to the universe): "I REALLY want _____."

So many of us fail to truly engage the Law of Attraction because we're afraid to hope and we're afraid to get our hopes dashed. I invite you let go of trying to protect yourself from disappointment.

The truth is: If you try to shield yourself from disappointment—disappointment in life will come anyway!

Instead, *decide now* to let yourself Want what you Want. Let go of having to know how you'll get your desire—instead acknowledge your deep desire and take appropriate action.

Now, will you always get what you want?

The answer is in three parts:

    a) sometimes you get what you want in exactly the

form you envision it
b) sometimes you get what you want in a BETTER form that you didn't imagine
c) sometimes you do not get what you want but you get something that deepens you as a human being so *you* become better.

Ginny and I parted ways after a time. But I continue to admire her spirit. She told me that she wanted to sing the lead role of Christine in *The Phantom of the Opera* musical. Alas, she was tone deaf. But I admired that she stayed in musical theater as a dancer.

And let's note this: What was her objective? – "I WANT to perform!"

And she got those opportunities over and over—as a dancer.

In summary, to raise your confidence level and to invoke the Law of Attraction do these things (along the lines of Ask, Believe, Receive):

- Find and acknowledge your objective [your "Want!"] and ASK.
- "Believe!"—that is envision how great you feel as if you are already receiving what you want
- Receive the blessing

A final comment about confidence:

I've done many things that scared me (directing feature films, guest-lecturing at Stanford University, acting as a lead actor in feature films). I've learned that my confidence did not rise from "comfort." No. It rose from my objective (deep desire), rehearsal, training, and from developing ways to be flexible and to adapt.

But the secret is: Confidence in my ability to adapt came from *the great personal energy provided by my Big*

Want.

I wanted something So Much that I put in the work (rehearsal, study, more) to do my best.

And each time, the Law of Attraction would give me blessings.

Principle
Focus on what you want and use that energy for training and rehearsal.

Power Questions
What training/coaching could help you leap forward to more prosperity and abundance?

Action and the Law of Attraction

(I first released this below material at my blog: www.BeHeardandBeTrusted.com)

Imagine using the Law of Attraction and really improving your life! I'm not talking about just using the steps of "Ask, Believe, Receive." Why? Because a lot of people have started and stayed with "Ask, Believe, Receive" and they've been *really disappointed.*

Why did those three steps by themselves fail to produce the results people desperately crave? Consider a revision to "Ask, Believe, TAKE EFFECTIVE ACTION, Receive."

Sure, the Law of Attraction rests on "similar energies are drawn together." Hold positive thoughts and enjoy positive results.

Let's focus deeper on this. To say this in few words, many positive results have manifested for me with positive thoughts PLUS positive action. *[This is where the*

Law of Creation enhances how the Law of Attraction works in your life.]

One time, I took action to direct a feature film and this led to an unforeseen positive result. During that time, an opportunity arose for me to have a conversation on the set with an actor's father. The result? I was given a contact that led to over $251,253. Do you notice the details: if I didn't say YES to direct the film or if I did not *do* well in directing the film, I would not have had that crucial conversation!

So repeat with me: "Ask, Believe, TAKE EFFECTIVE ACTION, Receive."

I invite you to ask yourself: "Where am I *not* taking action? What small action can I take so that I can start the flow of positive opportunities in my direction? Then, do MORE than have positive thoughts: Take Positive Action.

Recently, in a class, I replied to a question by saying, "I'm an Opti-Realist. Take your optimism plus realism and then you can win."

When I say "win," I mean enjoy success, joy and fulfillment. Often, there can be multiple winners. In my work, there can be multiple effective speakers, authors and producers. I realize that in the world of sports, there is one gold medalist for a particular sport. However, much of what we do provides us with opportunities beyond being "one winner." And thank goodness!

So let's return to "Ask, Believe, TAKE EFFECTIVE ACTION, Receive." The universe is waiting to see if you're serious about something. Will you study, rehearse, or get coaching? And will you "put yourself into the arena"? That is, will you go make the presentation to potential investors? Will you ask a person for a date? Will you complete your book and see that it's available on

Amazon?

Recently, a friend said, "It's not about wishing for more money, it's about saying a prayer that you become better at what you do. Then more money comes in naturally."

From that conversation, I coined a phrase: "It's not about asking for gifts; it's about increasing your capacity." That is, increase your capacity to effectively serve others, and the universe will naturally bring rewards and opportunities to you. You are then attractive. Now, that's the Law of Attraction in action!

Principle
Use action [the Law of Creation] to enhance how the Law of Attraction works in your life.

Power Questions
What small action can you take to move in the direction of your dreams?

Handle Anger through the Law of Attraction

Would you like less trouble and anger in your life? Fortunately, through certain actions and the Law of Attraction you can become skilled at dealing with anger.

First, I'm going to get to the heart of the matter: *Anger arises from fear.* In previous books, I've written that "Anger is fear twisted."

I've learned that if I'm angry, I am likely afraid that something bad is happening or is going to happen. I am concerned that someone I love will get hurt or I'll get hurt.

For example, many years ago, someone smashed into

the little Toyota truck that my sweetheart had borrowed from her parents.

That night, I was shocked that a big Ford F-150 truck backed into and crushed the end of the *parked,* little Toyota truck. The F-150 truck backed up and slammed into the little truck a *second time.*

I was scared for my sweetheart's feelings. She would be distraught: A hit-and-run vehicle would leave my sweetheart at odds with her parents.

So I immediately ran toward the offending vehicle that was seeking to *leave the scene.* Next thing, the F-150 truck hit me in the chest, and in desperation, I was clinging to the hood of the vehicle—the driver *still* trying to leave the scene.

I yelled for help, hoping someone in the Telegraph Hill neighborhood of San Francisco would hear me, somehow intervene, and call for the police!

This was the most *terrifying moment* of my life. I thought, "What will this crazy man do next? I'll be dead if I fall off and he runs me over. He might run me over on purpose!"

Finally, the police arrived and ultimately, after legal proceedings, compensation for the little Toyota truck came through. But was the cost of my jumping in front of the offender worth it?

One smashed little Toyota truck and an F-150 hitting me in the chest. Any ordinary person would brought the F-150 to a stop after the initial collision with the Toyota truck. But that didn't happen, and I put my life in unnecessary jeopardy.

My *fear* of my sweetheart being hurt, led to *my anger* and to my action.

Would I do the same thing now? No. Risking death-by-truck is *not* my style of living now!

Money can be replaced, not a human life.

* * *

Anger can lead to a bad reaction.

Instead, to really invoke the Law of Attraction, you want to be in a better state of being, one of calmness. From a state of calmness, you can respond in a thoughtful and wise manner.

Here's where the Law of Attraction also comes in. If you keep focusing on fear, you keep attracting things to be afraid about. Also, anger often involves being judgmental toward another person. We judge them as doing something wrong.

And by the Law of Attraction, the more we practice being judgmental—the more we attract judgmental people into our lives. Watch out for that!

So the solution is a combination of compassion and discernment.

When you live most of your day in compassion, you are in a calm state of being. In such a state, you can practice discernment.

Often when I talk with clients and my college students, the word *discernment* is not an immediate part of their vocabulary.

I'll make certain distinctions here:

Discernment: a flexible approach. You observe what works and what does *not*. Then, you make good decisions regarding your next actions.

Judgment: a rigid approach in which one sets oneself as superior to the other person.

Again, by the Law of Attraction, the more we practice

being judgmental, the more judgmental people we attract to us. Not good.

Instead, it's better to practice *discernment*. Do not settle for your instant, reflexive judgments about a person or situation.

Learn to practice shifting to a compassionate approach.

For example, as I type this into my mini-laptop, I'm being bumped by two things: a) the rocking of the train I'm traveling in and b) the annoying sounds of a married couple grumbling to each other. I can even hear the growling couple through the ear plugs that I'm wearing.

Wife: Oh, I spent that money.
Husband: You spent it on yourself [with a pushy tone]
Wife: Yeah.
Husband: On *personal* things.

Now, my instant thoughts include: "Why is it bad to spend money on yourself? Doesn't this guy know that it's good to nurture yourself? By the way, his cross-examining his wife is not smart. He is not honoring her."

But immediately, I remind myself to be compassionate. Maybe this couple is working their way through a process. Maybe they need to *talk through* money expenditures because they've gone through *some money troubles* recently.

In any case, I remind myself that I do not know them and we humans are just trying to do the best we can, with what we know in the moment.

This example illustrates another point: it's true that we can often shift to being kind and compassionate toward a stranger, but if a loved one does something that is hurtful—it hurts double! And we often get angry.

Why? Family members are supposed to know us, and so our expectations in how we're treat are more sensitive.

We have thoughts like: "You're my brother, you're supposed to be good to me!"

With compassion, however, we can view the situation as: "I prefer you to be kind to me, but you may be hurting so much (or you may be confused) that I'm *not* really in your mind at the moment. There is no room to think about how this situation affects me."

Years ago, Richard Carlson, author of *Don't Sweat the Small Stuff*, told me, "It's not that I don't get stressed out. It's that I do NOT spend much time there."

Similarly, it is good for us to learn to spend more of our day in a mode of compassion and discernment—and then we're likely to avoid pouring gasoline on small fires of irritation. In this way, we avoid igniting big flames of anger.

In a way, anger can be something that we "practice." In order to avoid, getting angry, it helps to practice something opposite: the calmness of compassion.

We do that by conditioning ourselves with compassionate thoughts.

Here are examples:

Judgmental Thought: That guy is being stupid.

Compassionate Thought: I don't know him. Maybe he's getting a divorce and he's distraught.

Judgmental Thought: That person is talking loud in his own language.

Compassionate Thought: Maybe that person has had some hearing loss. I bet my language sounds strange to him, too.

Judgmental Thought: What a mean thing to say!

Compassionate Thought: Maybe my family member is not trying to be mean. Maybe she's just tired.

Remember, to really get the Law of Attraction flowing well in your life, spend more of your day in a compassionate state of being.

Principle
When judgmental thoughts arise, shift to discernment, be flexible and make good choices.

Power Questions
What are some judgmental thoughts you have often? What would help you make a shift in your thoughts? Taking a breath? (Perhaps, you might tell yourself: "I shift from judgment to discernment.")

Handle Loss through the Law of Attraction

Some people are concerned that they're not "doing it right" if they experience grief when loss befalls them.

Actually—when grief occurs, it can happen because the Law of Attraction brought you high quality friends or high quality projects.

Of course, if a friend dies or another friend drifts away, it's supposed to hurt because you had something *valuable* in your life!

So how do you deal with grief in a "Law of Attraction friendly way"?

You learn to flow from moment to moment.

You avoid staying stuck.

On a given day, you may experience tears a number of times. Each time may be for part of an hour. And still, a few moments may actually bring you some instants of laughter.

Good! *You're stepping into each moment fresh.*

Some years ago, I was teaching a class of graduate students and I choked up. Just the day before, I learned that a close friend had committed suicide.

So I said to the students, "A close friend of mine has died. I might get choked up for 30 seconds. But things are okay. We'll flow forward soon."

Everything worked out. I even saw some students nod. They connected with me person to person.

The universe wants to bring you more friends and more projects.

So show the universe that you welcome it all: the joys, the highs, the lows and the grief when necessary.

Stay in the moment and remember to turn the direction of your thoughts by saying, "I'm grateful for _____." Fill in the blank with whatever warms your heart.

About projects: it's natural to feel some emptiness when a good project comes to completion.

The solution is to "overlap projects." Start another project *before* the ending of your current project. In this way you avoid a big dip in energy as you grieve over the ending of the first project.

Remember, step into each moment fresh.

Principle
Handle loss by learning to keep "in the flow."

Power Questions
How can you enter each moment fresh? Are you getting enough sleep? Do you take good care of yourself? Do you allow yourself to "feel it all"—to feel the joy, the

sorrow, and the love?

Handle Disappointment through the Law of Attraction

Have you thought that if you "did the Law of Attraction right" that you could avoid disappointment? I can help with this perception.

Every person who has had a major impact on world culture has endured BIG disappointments.

Thomas Edison's first patent yielded a product that the Congress shunned. He designed a device that could record a senator's vote quickly. But the Congress did NOT want that! They wanted to do backroom deals instead. So Edison faced big disappointment. Historians have said that this led to Edison always searching for a target market *first* before sinking effort and funds into a project.

Steve Jobs once tried to sell a computer named Lisa. People said that it cost too much and it did too little. The Lisa computer just disappeared into history without notice.

Walt Disney's first two companies went bankrupt.

Several years ago, Oprah Winfrey lost her new broadcasting anchor position because she reported the news with "too much emotion." That was a big disappointment for her!

Then she landed the host position for a show called "People Are Talking," and she said, "It was like coming home."

Oprah's TV program "The Oprah Winfrey Show" remains the highest-rated talk show in American television history. It did well for 25 seasons.

More recently, the debut of Oprah's cable channel OWN debuted to terrible ratings. In fact, she said that she was embarrassed to give a speech at Harvard University around that time. She felt like she was really failing. As of 2012 the OWN channel's losses were estimated as $330 million. Let's remember that Oprah is a billionaire, so she can take the hit, but the loss still hurts.

Oprah is likely to improve the network or do something different. I am *not* worried for her.

My point is: Doing the Law of Attraction "right" is NOT about avoiding all disappointment. *It's about attracting the experiences and resources that make you strong and truly capable of making great decisions at a particular time.*

If you feel big disappointment, some of those experiences are based on when you had something really good and then it went away.

Two of my friendships ended and I still grieve about them—when I think about them. But I am grateful that those friendships enhanced earlier chapters of my life

You see *I did have the Law of Attraction working well in my life:* I attracted those two friendships at *just the right time* to be good to those people—and they were kind to me.

To make this clear:

When the Law of Attraction is working well in your life, it's about JUST THE RIGHT TIME. You attract what you need for this chapter in your life. Sure things will change in later months or years. And you can feel disappointed. And that is okay. Not fun. But appropriate for one's journey in life.

As one of my editors suggested: "Sometimes losing something, like a friend who cuts you down, is a *good* thing!"

Be observant to see the big picture. And look for opportunities to say, "I am grateful for _____."

This keeps the Law of Attraction flowing well in your life.

Principle

Look at the big picture and frequently say, "I am grateful for _____."

Power Questions

What is working in your life? What are you grateful for? What gratitude-practice can you implement in your life? (You might want to list three positive details/occurrences from your day in a Gratitude Journal just before you go to sleep each night.)

The Law of Attraction and Your Feeling Good!

Do you remember a time when you felt great!? Some of us are out of practice in terms of feeling good.

Does this sound like you? Are you all clogged up with worrying and being busy?

Good moments can arrive but we may not make space for them. For example, a moment ago I was brushing my teeth getting ready to go to bed.

But then some ideas for this section leapt into my mind. Did I shrug and let the opportunity to write these words evaporate? No! I leapt to the computer and started typing. *And I feel great.*

Also, I know what images instantly put me in a good

mood. For example, I always feel good when I arrive outside Disneyland and see the top of the Matterhorn Mountain—visible above the trees that obscure the park from the street. It always reminds me: "I'm here at Disneyland!"

To really get the Law of Attraction working well, you need to become clear within your own self. In a way, you are "aiming" the Law of Attraction on your behalf. In fact, that's part of the "ask, believe, receive" idea within the Law of Attraction. *You need to ask for what you want.*

Here's another idea about feeling good. You need to look for *many ways* that will likely get you what you want.

For example, at this time, I don't have the opening in my schedule to be in Disneyland each month. However, when I walk down the main street of a nearby California town, I feel good. Why? This town has lights in their trees (just like Disneyland's Main Street U.S.A.)! So when I'm walking in that town, I can make a switch in my mind and look upon the world in a special way: seeing the magic.

I now invite you to write down in your journal those moments you have enjoyed.

My clients have noted:
- listening to music
- swing dancing
- tai chi
- reading a good book

Remember, do you homework. To really have the Law of Attraction flowing in your life, learn what you really like and what gets you to feel good.

In this way, your "message to the universe" will be clear, "I'll have more of these magic moments, please. Thank you!"

Principle
To attract more times when you feel good, identify what you enjoy doing and experiencing.

Power Questions
Can you recall some of the moments in your life when you felt good? How could you bring moments like these into your present life?

* * *

Now that I've talked about your feeling good, here are Molly Nece's insights on bringing more joy and fulfillment to your life.

Live *Your* 5 P Philosophy
by Molly Nece

After 39 years on earth, if I knew then what I know now, there may have been a few less zigs and zags along the way, but I am grateful for the extra adventures it has caused. My guess is twenty years from now I will be saying the same thing. That said, if I had a few less paths traveled, I may not be as impactful in the services I provide and the people I serve. That said, I would like to share with you something I have come to call the 5 P Philosophy. It has enabled me to know when I'm out of alignment and need to stop, reflect, and shift. After all, we are all mere mortals.

The 5 P's are as follows—principles, passions, people, persistence, and peace. Being aware of what is important to you will help to guide all future decisions and help to strengthen and nurture relationships with the third P—People. For example, my principles are health, family, helping, adventure, and economic serenity. If I am not getting the sleep my body requires, not drinking enough water, and doing too much left-brain paperwork at my desk, it starts to show in my communication style and energy level. In my book, *The 5 P Philosophy*, you can take the principle quiz for yourself. I also recommend those you spend the most time with take it too. For instance, one of my husband's top five core principles is pride/self-respect. Early in our marriage I had to adjust my communication style because my words were triggering his emotional intelligence. Plus, looking back, I could take ownership for some of my poor choice of words. Our relationship is stronger because of this awareness and vulnerability we both chose to explore and continue to explore throughout our marriage.

The next 'P' is passion. I knew what I did and didn't like to do and how much I could tolerate doing what I didn't like to do and what part of the day I should take on the most undesirable tasks. I also realized that with enough persistence and a can-do attitude that I would strike a happy medium between my day job and hobby that will eventually become my fulltime job. In life, there is no space in the brain for what I call "monkeys in the brain." They run around and take you off your ultimate vision of success. There were plenty of opportunities for monkeys to enter my brain, but I knew that it was me who controlled my thoughts, words, and actions. It was my duty to keep aware and persistent in achieving goals that led to living out my passions to the fullest. You must believe that one passion puzzle piece will lead to the next.

The third 'P' is people. There are a few people you may

need to kick off your bus. It may be a little lonely for a while until you attract those you are seeking, but soon there will be people clamoring to get on the bus because of the brand you have chosen to build in spite of or because of. Always keep front of mind who you want to do business with and who you want to serve on your personal and professional board of directors. Don't forget to look for ways to serve others. When you spend an equal, if not more time, giving than taking, you end up filling up your heart, mind, and eventually your bank account. Another wisdom is that learning doesn't stop in college. If you are smart, you will continue to seek knowledge and look for ways to apply it. This is one of the reasons I decided to get my Lean Six Sigma and Mediation Certificate. In other words, ABL... Always be learning!

The forth 'P' is persistence. So often people think fame and fortune happen over night. The problem is they don't mix the persistence and peace together in their efforts. Peace is the final 'P.' People will say they are working hard, but is it on the tasks that will have them reap the reward they have specifically defined? Most of the people I coach are extremely hard working, but are not tracking the success of their efforts or identifying what success looks like prior to putting all the sweat equity into the process. Once peace is defined, they adjust and immediately begin to experience more success and satisfaction at work and in life.

Molly Nece has spent over fifteen years in corporate and higher education administration. Ten of those years have been focused in the field of training and organizational development. Over the past five years, she has enjoyed building two training companies and writing six books. Molly has received her Master's in Training and Organizational Development from West Chester University; Bachelor's degrees in Psychology and Elementary Education from Gettysburg College; and two certificates—Lean Six Sigma from Villanova and Mediation from Lakewood College.

Her vast knowledge is supported with real-life stories and hands on activities that help to motivate her audiences to take action. As a result of her experiences in leadership, service, team strengthening, and productivity, she has gained valuable insight that equips her clients to succeed in both good and challenging economies. Because of these vast and varied experiences, she enjoys helping private, public, non-profit, and religious groups create goldmines both at work and home through The Nece Group. To learn more about how she can help inspire and equip you and your teams to peak performance, go to www.TheNeceGroup.com.

Have Some Targets and the Law of Attraction Helps You Reach Them

Below I'm including one of my articles from my blog at www.BeHeardandBeTrusted.com.

This particular blog article arose from my intuition and a strange experience I lived through. This relates to the Law of Attraction in that *we need to have some real targets in order for the Law of Attraction operate well in our lives."*

"I was Tweeted by a Dead Man" and Insights on Life

A tweet from Joe?! I was shocked. He had been dead over a month. Joe's Hollywood business manager had alerted me to Joe's passing after I had called Joe repeatedly but had only heard his outgoing voicemail message.

Joe's business manager assured me that police officers had entered Joe's home and found him dead.

But still I received a tweet. I studied the tweet and realized that it was likely Joe's Twitter account was somehow connected to a feed from another person's account. I admit that I felt a gut-punch of grief on realizing that Joe really was gone.

I know a couple of people who have died but their Facebook wall remains visible. Now, on a deceased person's wall, you can see "R.I.P" (rest in peace) in messages left by bereaved loved ones.

You can see what the dead person was posting and commenting on in their last days of life.

Yesterday, I finished reading *Jim Henson: The Biography*—a good book. The leader behind the success of the Muppets died at 53 years old.

Do you think about your legacy? Who will remember you? What good will outlive you?

This is important.

At one point, a guy I'll call "Stephen" told me about how upset he was with God. Stephen had attended all the services and done all of the rituals required by his religion. But Stephen was *not* getting what he wanted. He was mad!

I then had a thought. I said to Stephen, *"Maybe, you need someone new to serve."*

(In recent years, Stephen had been isolating himself. He was not engaged with people and so his life was bereft of the *blessings of good feelings that people have when they're being helpful to others.*)

Researchers have verified that people tend to feel better when they feel valuable to the lives of others.

I invite you to find some way to be helpful to others.

For example, my company Tom Marcoux Media, LLC holds to this mission: *"We create energizing, encouraging edutainment for our good and humankind's rise."*

You don't need to have a company to focus on service.

Stay observant, and listen to your intuition.

For example, this morning, I woke up with the thought that I had not finished reading the book, *The Disneyland Encyclopedia*.

Later, I walked into a particular room and happened to find the book in a pile of other books.

Then I read a paragraph in this book that included a mention of "Sam," someone I know.

I thought about sending Sam an email and telling him the good news that he and his one-man show were referenced in the book.

Then, I opened my email and found a note from Linkedin.com that alerted me that *today is Sam's birthday*. So I sent him a happy birthday message that included the "gift" of telling him that he is referenced on page 101.

I shared the above example to demonstrate that we can all be kind and of service to each other—everyday.

Take good care of yourself and listen to your intuition. Watch for opportunities to be helpful.

Make your life count.

Let kindness be your legacy.

And, you'll enjoy your life today!

Principle

Find ways to be of service to people and let kindness be your legacy.

Power Questions

How can you be supportive of someone each day? Will

you send helpful Internet links or something else to nurture your network of contacts?

Enhance the Blessings of the Law of Attraction — when You Improve Your "Verbal Reflexes"

"No, it won't work."

"No, I can't do that."

Do you know someone who says comments like the two above? Do you find yourself falling into reflexive comments that are negative and that drain you of energy?

I know a number of people so negative that they do not even notice the energy-draining drivel pouring from their mouths. It's like a *reflex*.

They say things like "Oh! I'm so stupid!"

"That driver is an a__h___!"

Some older people have told me, "Oh, that's not really a problem. It doesn't matter."

However, it *does* matter in two important ways:
- You drain your own energy
- You attract more negative things to you daily

1) You drain your own energy.

By the Law of Attraction, when you're judgmental and cruel toward yourself, you attract other people who are judgmental and cruel!

Why? It feels "like home." If cruelty is what you endured while growing up, it's likely that love and cruelty become twisted together. It even feels "safe" because it's familiar.

The point here is: Being reflexively negative with your

words can literally drain you of energy. In many ways, there are no "neutral words." Words either build you up or tear you down.

Surround yourself with only people who are going to lift you higher. - Oprah Winfrey

Who are you around the most? YOU.

So be sure that your reflexive ways of talking build you up.

I've worked with clients with horrible, reflexive words and self-assessments.

The self-criticizers make a mistake and say: "I'm so stupid. I always f--- up. No wonder no one likes me."

On the other hand, the successful people I've interviewed say: "I made a mistake. I take responsibility. I'll do better next time. Looks like I need some coaching and rehearsal here. Okay. I've learned something."

You can see that the successful people are *coaching* themselves to do better! They don't waste time or energy on pointless self-abuse.

Realize:

Your habitual ways of talking either build you up or tear you down.

2. You attract more negative things to you daily

The rules of the Law of Attraction emphasize that what you focus on you get *more* of.

So those people who call themselves "clumsy" and klutz" attract more accidents. They keep *proving* to themselves that they are what they claim to be!

On the other hand, for years, I have purposely chosen to say, "I have an excellent memory."

For example, in a new class of college students, I call roll call and I'll celebrate that I get 22 out of 25 student's names correct during the second class.

The self-criticizer will emphasize the 3 mistakes.

Instead, I emphasize the 22 correct actions! I tell myself: "See I *do* have a good memory."

A number of authors suggest that "Life is something we co-create with God." If that's true, why would anyone want to set up a negative self-fulfilling prophesy? *Stop that.*

I once was appalled at how two generations in a family told themselves a bad story and called it the "Brown Family Bad Luck."

They said that they were in a van, the father was driving, and their van's tire suffered a blowout.

"On the freeway?" I asked.

"No, on the off-ramp."

"Anyone get hurt?"

"No. Anyway, it's our usual bad luck that we had a blowout."

I thought: "Wait a minute. Don't these people realize how lucky they were to have the blowout on *the off ramp* and to come to *safe stop*?! No other car hit them."

The problem here is: The two parents and grown children kept telling themselves the same story of "bad luck."

That's *the opposite* of correctly enhancing the blessings of the Law of Attraction in your life. Instead, tell all of the good stories.

* * *

Take conscious choice of how *you* influence your own life. Choose your habitual words carefully. Stop cutting yourself down. Stop telling yourself "bad luck" stories.

See each blessing you have enjoyed. Tell stories about those blessings.

Lift yourself up. Coach yourself positively.

Principle
Train yourself to talk in ways that build you up.

Power Questions
What habitual sayings/stories do you express that cut you down? How can you replace such downer items with something that empowers you?

Handle Fear—
and The Law of Attraction Enhances Your Life

When you handle fear and stop it from overrunning your life, the Law of Attraction can operate with more power in your favor.

A number of authors suggest that if you think about what you fear most of the time, you'll attract more of what you fear.

The solution for this situation is: Train Yourself to shift your thoughts.

It can be a simple as: "I'm afraid of having trouble during my upcoming speech. *What do I need to do well?* Who can listen to me rehearse? Can I glance at a couple of books?*"

The idea is to shift from fear to *"something I can do."*

[* If you'd like a free report "9 Deadly Mistakes to Avoid for Your Next Speech and 9 Surefire Methods" — go to http://tomsupercoach.com/freereport9Mistakes4Speech.html]

For more about dealing with fear and self-doubt, we will now view a reprint of an article from my blog:

Get More Done Even when Hit with Self-Doubt and Criticism

Like a punch to my stomach, the statement from an official of the San Luis Obispo Airport rang in my ears, "You need to get your film crew out of here." We'd been filming for only one hour. As the producer-director of my first feature film, I knew that we were promised three hours.

I didn't waste a moment. I said, "Fine. We're leaving." I told my co-producer, "Have the extras leave the area. But have them walk slowly. As we go along, I'll have crew remove some movie lights." I kept filming and acting in shots while the official watched equipment and people leave. Twenty minutes later, it came down to me and one cameraman. And then we were done.

My intuition the day before yelled at me: "They might renege on the 3-hour plan." So I moved forward by storyboarding the most important shots and planned to do them first—the shots with the American Eagle airplane and the lead actors running after the plane. My intuition served me well. I listened to my gut.

Reality includes people reneging on a plan and others criticizing what you do. What's worse are the negative "voices" in our heads that bury us in self-doubt.

What's the difference that high-achievers/successful people have that people-who-are-stuck don't have? **It is the practice of stepping forward regardless of self-doubt and criticism.**

"Self-doubt is like a puppy you tuck under your arm before running across a six-lane highway." – Steve Chandler

Okay. I'm **NOT** an advocate for running across a highway. But I do see the point: *We take appropriate risks and just carry that little puppy of self-doubt with us.*

I find the above quote to inspire my freedom. Why? Because I do NOT wait for self-doubt to disappear. I press on anyway. I get coaching and I do necessary preparations and rehearsal. I say, "Courage is easier when you're prepared."

I've noticed a number of people who get stuck because they're waiting for self-doubt or lack of confidence to go away.

Do NOT let yourself to get stuck in that trap.

We'll use the N.O.W. process:

N – notice the next step and do it

O – open to coaching

W – write YOUR story

1. Notice the next step and do it

When I prepared to produce, write and direct my first feature film, I was scared. What if the film does not work? What if the crew thinks I'm too green and do not follow my directions to move fast? (Low budget filmmaking requires the team to move fast because there are so few days of filming.)

The important detail is to **Take the Next Step.**

It was easy to project into the future—that's where all of the fear lies in wait. What if the film does not turn out? What if I can't get a distributor?

Stop all of that. *Focus on the next step.* The next step is to finish the first draft of the script. Later, before the first day of filming, my next step was to personally draw 801 storyboards (illustrations). I knew exactly how one scene would transition into the next scene. I also storyboarded the complicated action scenes. How do you film landing a jets ski into the bed of a speeding truck? I figured details out in advance.

Do *not* wait to feel comfortable.

Plan your next step and take action.

2. Open to coaching

I have seen a number of episodes of the TV Show, *Restaurant Impossible*. Chef Robert Irvine arrives at a restaurant that is failing and coaches the owners to massively change their menu, working methods, leadership actions—and the restaurant gets a fantastic visual makeover!

The restaurant owners who get the most benefit are those *Open to Coaching*. The truth is they would not need Chef Robert Irvine to intervene if they really knew the best practices. Many of the restaurant owners never even worked in someone else's restaurant! How would they know what are best practices?

A phrase I use often with clients is "ALF – adapt, learn, flex."

In order to improve, we need to acknowledge that we possess weaknesses and then get coaching to improve. We will learn, adapt and flex our options. More than that, a good coach will guide us to measure our daily activities towards improvement.

"Measurement is the first step that leads to control and eventually to improvement. If you can't measure something, you can't understand it. If you can't understand it, you can't control it. If you can't control it, you can't improve it."

— H. James Harrington

I have a number of Project Logs. I note how many words a day I write and also how many pages of the trilogy of *Jack AngelSword* (graphic novels) are completed.

I invite you to get coaching, and I applaud that you're reading these words and giving me the honor to coach you at the moment.

3. Write YOUR story

Perhaps, you noticed something strange like I have. The people who yell the loudest have no experience in doing what they're criticizing.

Many times, I have taken risks to live out adventures. I have lived as an actor, lead singer/song writer, model, feature film director, guest instructor at Stanford University and more. Yet people who have never attempted such activities, threw their *negative advice* at me.

I learned to listen to my heart more than their criticisms.

It was MY story. Not their story. It was NOT their IMAGINED ideas of how to do things better, but MY ideas of how to do things better.

With my college students, I suggest: "Seek the advice of someone who has *accomplished* what you want to accomplish."

And still, you will find your OWN way of doing things.

I've reached a point where I'm comfortable in my own skin, and I do what I need to do, to feel good, but I'm built the way I am. The dancer's feet, the bruises on my legs, they're not going to go away. I think real girls have bruises. Tough chicks get bruised. They get dirty. And they have fun. - Nina Dobrev

By the way, I recall completing a film and my then-girlfriend said, "I've never seen a film like this." Okay, then. Perhaps, it works for you or it doesn't.

I find that the very things that I get criticized for, which is usually being different and just doing my own thing and just being original, is the very thing that's making me successful.

- Shania Twain

Sometimes, family members criticize what we're doing, not because they're helping us, it's because *they* do not want to feel uncomfortable. The truth is: We all get our share of disappointment. Successful people get even more disappointment because they're trying more things. Follow your heart—and get useful coaching along the way.

I learned a long time ago the wisest thing I can do is be on my own side, be an advocate for myself . . . - Maya Angelou

So I invite you to press forward even if you're criticized, even if you have self-doubt.

Take the next step.

Principle
Listen to your heart more than criticism.

Power Question
How can you remind yourself of your "first heartfelt intention." regarding a project or course of action?

The Law of Attraction and the "3 C's of Success"

One of my speech topics is "Power Up the 3 C's of Success: Charisma, Confidence and Control of Time."

Now I'll share how the Law of Attraction relates to the

3 C's.

I summarize the 3 C's as

Charisma – They trust you

Confidence – You believe in you.

Control of Time – You get the most important things done; you do NOT procrastinate. And people trust this!

1. Charisma

I've talked with a number of people who say that they think charisma is something that one is "born with."

When talking with my college level, public speaking students, I note: "What we call charisma is often just referring to what I call *Magnetic Charisma*. Perhaps, the charisma of a young President Bill Clinton or Angelina Jolie. **There's more to charisma than that.**"

I go on to note:

Natural Charm Charisma: This is a form of charisma that comes easier to a person. For example, some people are not extroverts in their speech, but they're terrific listeners.

Warm Trust Charisma: This is the form of charisma that gains cooperation. People trust the charismatic person.

How Charisma Enhances the Law of Attraction in Your Life:

Specifically, with Warm Trust Charisma, people feel comfortable in your presence. You place them at ease. When they are comfortable and trusting, they're more likely to give you referrals and bring opportunities to you. It's not just who you know; it's about: *Do they trust you?*

You can enhance the Law of Attraction working in your favor with these trustworthy behaviors:

a) You fulfill your promises.

b) If something changes, you let people know quickly.

c) You avoid saying "yes" too much. (It's better to politely say 'no,' than to say 'yes' and later disappoint someone.)

d) You are a little early for all appointments.

e) You look out for the well-being of other people.

2. Confidence

In another part of this book, I speak of "ALF – adapt, learn, flex."

Here's the truth: Confidence is *not* about feeling comfortable.

I've given speeches with 723 people in the audience and networked at Stanford University and IBM. I was not fully comfortable during those times, but I believed in my rehearsal and preparation. I knew I could adapt and flex. Every speech has been a learning process for me, and each time I continue to improve because I adapt, learn and flex.

The confidence I possess is because of my diligent and intentional application of ALF (adapt, learn and flex) in every situation and challenge that presents itself in my life.

How Confidence Enhances the Law of Attraction in Your Life:

Simply put, confidence attracts. Why? All of us are aware of our own fears. It's great to be around someone who reassures us. Nelson Mandela later confessed that during the time he was in prison, he *was* afraid. But he did *not* reveal his fear to the other prisoners. In this way, the other prisoners were reassured.

So your confidence reassures others.

It's possible to feel some jitters in your gut, and still give a great speech. I've seen my clients and graduate students do that many times.

Get coaching and rehearse.

3. Control of Time

Let's face it: You'll do better when you attract people who *respect your time*. An old phrase is: "You teach people how to treat you."

Show people how you value time, and how you value *their* time. Arrive a bit early for appointments. Furthermore, do the most important things.

For example, my clients and I practice: "Worst first."

We identify the tough task (the "worst first") and do it *first*.

This practice drops much procrastination from your life. People then trust you. And you're attractive for more opportunities.

Principle:

The Law of Attraction favors people who have worked to enhance their 3 C's: Charisma, Confidence and Control of Time.

Power Questions:

How can you practice more behaviors that inspire people to trust you?

How can you rehearse before tough events?

How can you focus your attention on "Worst first"?

* * *

Many of us can enhance our charisma and influence by

honing our speaking skills. Now, Craig Harrison provides insights about communicating well.

Your Audience Speaks. Are You Listening?
By Craig Harrison

Try to decipher what you "hear" from your audience, what it means and what you can do about it.

As speakers we naturally believe that our audiences should listen to us. But how well are we listening to our audience? Believe it or not, that's the key to really connecting with an audience.

It may surprise you to learn that your audience speaks. I don't mean the whispering and side conversations that may occur during your speech. I mean the feedback they give you, the speaker, with facial expressions, body posture and attentiveness, throughout your presentation. Applause isn't the only time one can "listen" to their audience.

Listen *Before* You Speak
Prior to being introduced for your presentation, what do you hear from the audience? Are they restless, listless, or something in between? Are the people in the back making noise, the people in the sunlight getting drowsy? Has the previous speaker or activity lulled them into a state of complacency? Are they already psyched up from a previous discussion or interchange? I've been at events where a provocative business debate has left people on edge, or when a spirited Q&A session left members on the upbeat. Once my speech followed a hypno-therapist. I just

wish she'd restored our audience to their "original upright position."

Take the tenor of your audience *before* you approach the podium. Note their state. You may wish to alter your remarks or the way you deliver them so as to better connect with your audience. You can even tell your introducer to "rev the audience up" a little more if they are down, or to tone down your introduction if your audience is already flying high and your topic requires serious reflection.

Be "In The Moment"

Most speakers I know prepare extensively, including visualizing their speech opening prior to their arrival at the podium that day. Yet when you are introduced and look out at your actual audience, you should not be completely on auto-pilot. Take a moment to gauge your audience's mood as you look out at them.

I've seen a speaker ask everyone to take a breath or two with him, so they could all begin refreshed. I've similarly seen speakers, as a change of pace, ask their audiences to close their eyes for a moment while the speaker paints a scene in their mind's eye, before continuing. This breaks any spell that lingered from a previous speaker or activity. I myself have asked audiences who have been sitting too long to stand up and take a fifteen second stretch break with me.

Sending and Receiving Information

Speaking isn't just a 'stand and deliver' proposition. Speaking involves your receiving information as well. Has your audience been properly predisposed to your presentation through the way you were introduced? Did attendees laugh or "ooh" or "ah" where you intended them to during your own opening? Can they hear you? Can they see you?

By "listening" to your audience you can determine whether all members of your audience can hear you, whether people in the back as well as the front can see you, and also whether your audience is tracking your presentation in other ways.

What do the faces of your audience look like? Are they relaxed? Are they nodding in agreement? Are they leaning forward, indicating they either can't hear you or are having trouble understanding you?

If you are using highly technical terms, speaking at a fast rate of speed, or possess a thick accent, your audience members may be expending additional effort to understand your speech and follow your train of thought. As you "hear" this from furrowed brows or members turning to each other to ask "what did she say?" or "what does that mean?" you should either clarify your statements, slow down, or strive to enunciate more clearly. Often, due to our time constraints, we're guilty of over-reliance on TLAs (three letter acronyms), jargon, or just trying to say too much in a short period of time. Especially in speeches, less is more.

Try to decipher what you "hear" from your audience, what it means, and then what you can do about it.

When the audience is fidgeting, they may be too hot. Lower the temperature in the room. Is their fidgeting due to other causes, perhaps owing to your topic or subject matter?

Is your topic or subject matter making them uncomfortable? Especially if this was unintended you should acknowledge that you see your remarks are having this unintended effect. Avoid "making your audience wrong" for their feelings or reactions to your presentation. They have a right to react in any way they wish. Perhaps you're touching a nerve. Your listening lets you know.

Some speakers will unintentionally divide their audience through their presentation. Whether you're competing in a contest or just trying to persuade your audience of your point of view, dividing your audience through polarizing remarks you make can undermine your efforts. Remarks that praise one group at another's expense part of your audience feeling smart, the other part just smarting from your remarks. Strive to speak to universal themes or find the common ground among your diverse audience for maximum success

Sound Advice on Humor

It's said humor is invoked for one of three purposes: as a shield to protect, as a sword to attack, or as a bridge to connect. Listen to your audience's response to determine if you are bringing your audience together, unifying and connecting them with your humor. If your humor is falling flat, you may be dividing your audience through humor that is only funny to part of the group: women or men, young or old, immature vs. mature, etc. Strive to use humor that all can revel in.

Another important key to humor: give your audience time to laugh! Use pauses to allow your humor to sink in. Your pauses send cues to your audience that they are encouraged to ponder your words, and react accordingly. If they aren't laughing, it may be because you're not allowing them the opportunity to laugh. Take a breath now and then and watch the laughter flow. If your speaking slot is rigidly timed, realize that the larger the audience you speak to, the longer the audience takes to laugh. Don't alienate your meeting planner or sponsor because the laughter deriving from your 7 minute speech previously delivered to a small audience now lasts a minute longer when more people laugh. Plan accordingly so you can listen to your audience's laughter without it disrupting your speech's timing.

Give Your Audience a Place in Your Presentation

Without your audience you're just talking to yourself. Make sure your presentation has a place in it for them, and not just through their laughter. Members of your audience want and need to be a part of your presentation. They need to be acknowledged, enjoy being involved and respect a speaker that respects them. Help your audience find themselves within your presentation. *Listen* for opportunities for them to respond, react and be recognized and you will be listening to thunderous applause by speech's end. Whether you address certain members by name, acknowledge specifics of their experience, or reference previous events in the room, such customization within your presentation shows you've been listening, looking and learning about them and their experience. Audiences love that!

So the next time you speak to an audience, don't forget to listen to them too. They'll hear you better when you do!

The founder and principal of ExpressionsOfExcellence.com, **Craig Harrison** is an author, trainer, coach and speaker who builds competencies and confidence in employees of business enterprises ranging from start-ups to the Fortune 100. Craig's ability to instill passion about excellence in customer service helps his clients attract new customers, strengthen customer loyalty, improve internal morale and become customer service leaders in their industries. Craig has been featured in *The Wall Street Journal, The Financial Times, Selling Power* and *Business Week*. His clients include Bank of America, CIGNA, HP, Pfizer, Sheraton Hotels, Staples and United Airlines.

Visit www.ExpressionsOfExcellence.com,
e-mail Craig@ExpressionsOfExcellence.com
or call Craig directly at (510) 547-0664.

* * * * * *

When you're serious about unleashing the full potential of the Law of Attraction in your life, you'll take great care about focusing your thoughts and personal energy in a peaceful manner. Here are Jeanna Gabellini's insights about that process:

Peace is the Way
by Jeanna Gabellini

I've had several BIG aha moments in my life, **but the biggest transformation has come from a single focus … peace.**

You'd think that with a business name like Master Peace Coaching my focus would always be about being at peace. Not so. I get caught in the same traps as everyone else when it comes to getting results, relationships and letting go of the past. I find myself focusing on single (not usually tragic) problems rather than being present to the abundance right in front of my face.

This past week I was walking my daily route around the neighborhood and noticed a bright patch of green grass at the park behind my house. I stopped dead in my tracks and took a photo for you [on my blog].

Why?

Because for the past few months I've had internal conversations about the water drought in California causing the city to cut back on watering, which is killing the lawn at this normally lush park. I was bummed to see this beautiful spot go dry.

But that day my attention zeroed in on the one part of the lawn that looked really good. And I felt hope, appreciation, and abundance in that moment.

How often in your business do you zero in on all the areas that aren't working quickly enough? Or your mojo is crushed by that one person who didn't buy your offer, or walked out of your presentation? And have you ever made a sale but instead of celebrating you thought, "that's great but I need $XXXX more to make the bills?"

Here's my little trick to make a BIG transformation in your profits ... focus on peace. Make feeling at peace more important than making money, getting stuff done or getting it done right.

When I was at the worst period of my business (debt, no new clients and no new ideas to rescue it), nothing I did made a difference until I stopped trying so hard to make money. Being broke sucks, but the pressure I put on myself to turn it around was even worse. I felt helpless ... full of anxiety and judgment.

When I changed my focus to peace I felt empowered, in control and okay. When I wasn't focused on being broke I felt happy. I was living fully present to the resources and abundance around me. I still did the things I thought were good for my business, but I wasn't an emotional wreck in the process.

And that led to the business turnaround of the century.

Nine months later I was debt free, making six-figures and feeling like I was walking my talk.

I had the same thing happen with a food addiction in my thirties. I had coaches, books and tools to break through the pain but nothing worked … until I made my focus peace instead of getting rid of my addiction.

Once you make friends with peace, all of the great tools that failed you in the past may be of huge value in your transformation because you are now present to let it in.

So, peace, baby! Peace. That's the most important thing (besides fun!).

Jeanna Gabellini is a Master Business Coach who supports conscious entrepreneurs to double (and even triple) their profits by leveraging attraction principles, proven strategies and fun. She is also the co-author *of Life Lessons for Mastering the Law of Attraction*, with Eva Gregory, Mark Victor Hansen & Jack Canfield. And her newest book: *10 Minute Money Makers: How to Easily Double Your Profits in Just 10 Minutes a Day!*

Combining vision, divine guidance and easy to implement actions, Jeanna delivers top-tier private coaching & sold-out seminars that have allowed committed entrepreneurs to blow past their self-imposed limits, ditch the drama of overwhelm and move into radical joy, inner peace and ever-increasing profits.

www.MasterPEACEcoaching.com

* * * * * *

Really leaping forward in life involves two things in particular, the Law of Attraction *and* the Law of Creation. You might attract the best instruction and coaching, but if you do not take action and *create* with what you've learned, you'll remain stuck. Now Jeanna Gabellini provides key ideas about moving forward.

New Strategy Phobia
by Jeanna Gabellini

When I want something, I immediately go into action to get what I want. I don't do a bunch of research. I'm inspired and excited so I get my rear in gear.

This is not always the best way to be when choosing a new financial investment or choosing new strategies to build a business. I've been burned countless times because I didn't stop to ask myself how the strategy fit into my plan. I also never took the time to research what it would take to fully utilize the strategy for success.

Over time I became skeptical of trying new systems, strategies and technologies in my business. I didn't want to be that person who jumped on every new thing the experts promised would make me a million dollars … and wind up broke and disappointed.

As usual, swinging from one side of a perspective to another doesn't solve your issues. I missed out on tons of awesome resources that my peers were using to uplevel their businesses. I made up a story that I wasn't smart enough to implement those same strategies in a way that got rockstar results.

After many years, I decided I'd had enough of "New Strategy Phobia."

Now when I hear a peer raving about something new they are using to improve their business, I ask questions. I ask about the cost to implement it, the statistics, their overall strategy and what was involved to create a system around it.

Some people try all the latest 'whiz bang' strategies and talk about how amazing it is **BEFORE** they get results. In the past, I listened to those people because it was verrrry easy for me to jump on board based on their enthusiasm.

Other people test their strategies before they brag. Those are the people I listen to now. And then I still do some research, ask how it fits into my plan and implement with care and attention.

Another important question: Am I willing to do what it takes to keep the strategy or system working well?

During my last launch I installed a chat feature on one of my sales pages. Once installed, we planned for success. Who would man the chat line? How would I know if someone wanted to chat? Who would teach me how to use it?

My team and I created a system to handle this feature. My manager figured out how it worked and gave me a quick tutorial. We decided that I'd man the chat line when I was not on calls and she'd do it when I was busy. I made a Post-it note to remind me to turn on the system when I walked into my office each morning.

The chat feature was directly responsible for **over $10,000 in sales** during my launch. And it was fun chatting with the potential customers! The system to implement this new feature was critical for my success.

I also tried another new strategy during my launch that scared the pants off me … Facebook ads! Several of my peers had been bragging about this for almost a year.

I immediately discounted it …
- It'll cost too much money.
- I'd have to figure out the 'perfect' ad.
- How would I track the sales?
- That's for big-time marketers who have money to burn.

- Seems complicated. Too much to learn.

My friend, Justin, was getting phenomenal results with Facebook and he offered to teach me his formula. He does lots of testing before he shares his strategies. Guess what? **I made almost $5,000 of pure profit my first week using it, from people not previously on my email list! Happy dance!**

This is a strong nudge to try a new strategy in the next week. Do some research, make sure it's aligned with your plan and have some fun. May the results surprise and delight you!

Jeanna Gabellini is a Master Business Coach who supports conscious entrepreneurs to double (and even triple) their profits by leveraging attraction principles, proven strategies and fun. She is also the co-author of *Life Lessons for Mastering the Law of Attraction*, with Eva Gregory, Mark Victor Hansen & Jack Canfield. And her newest book: *10 Minute Money Makers: How to Easily Double Your Profits in Just 10 Minutes a Day!*

Combining vision, divine guidance and easy to implement actions, Jeanna delivers top-tier private coaching & sold-out seminars that have allowed committed entrepreneurs to blow past their self-imposed limits, ditch the drama of overwhelm and move into radical joy, inner peace and ever-increasing profits.

www.MasterPEACEcoaching.com

* * * * * *

In some cases, the Law of Attraction is the beginning, but taking powerful action is the *real springboard* to transforming your life for the better. Now Rebecca Morgan guides us on the crucial difference: taking action to make sure your follow-through is impeccable.

How's Your Follow Through?
by Rebecca Morgan, CSP, CMC

In my experience, lots of people say yes to things they never provide. Some people even volunteer to do something that never materializes. And they don't even have the professionalism to get back to the person or group to whom they committed to tell them they won't be delivering what was promised.

Two recent occurrences of this reminded me of how rampant this bad habit is.

• I ordered some special shoes from a store that specializes in shoes for difficult feet. I purposely went in 3 weeks before a trip abroad and was assured they would arrive before I left. When I hadn't heard anything 2 days before my trip, I called them and was told I would be called back the next day. I reminded the clerk of the time sensitivity and he assured me he'd get back to me before I left. He didn't.

After my trip I called again. I was told I'd be called the next day. I wasn't. This happened one more time, then I went into the store to talk to the manager. She said they'd been swamped. I said, "Then your people shouldn't promise things they can't fulfill." She nodded. I said it was all about managing expectations—that lying and saying you'll call back and then you don't is bad business. She nodded again.

Part of the problem is my expectation that merchants will actually do what they promise. I should know better and take my business to places that have proven their integrity and reliability. However, when expertise is in short supply, we put up with bad behavior. However, when the competition increases, few customers would put up with this lack of follow through.

- I'm remodeling my kitchen and gathered contractor recommendations from neighbors and friends. Most contractors called me back, but a few didn't. Of those who did, most made and kept appointments to look at the projects. They all promised proposals. About 80% of them sent those. Even when I followed up with the other 20%, they promised a proposal but I didn't receive one. I sent a thank you email to all those who sent a proposal, asking specific clarifying questions. Only about half responded.

Of the final 4, I asked for references. They all said they'd send names and numbers, but only one did. Guess who got the business?

Follow through is essential. It shows you're a professional and serious about wanting the business. If you know you can't provide something, don't promise it. If you promise something then find you can't deliver, let the person know. This makes you someone others want to work with, whether on internal projects, or with customers.

It takes diligence to track your promises, and a system to ensure you did what you said you would. But when you do, you'll stand out from those whose promises are empty. You'll show you're a true professional—one that others can count on.

Rebecca L. Morgan, CSP, CMC, specializes in creating innovative solutions for customer service challenges. She's appeared on *60 Minutes, Oprah, the Wall Street Journal, National Public Radio* and *USA Today*. Rebecca is the bestselling author of 25 books, including *Calming Upset Customers* and *Professional Selling*. She is an exemplary resource who partners with you to accomplish high ROI on your strategic customer service projects.

For information on her services, books, and resources, or for permission to repost or reprint this article, contact her at 408/998-7977, Rebecca@RebeccaMorgan.com, http://www.RebeccaMorgan.com

* * * * * *

When you really want to take a leap forward and make sure the Law of Attraction flows well in your life, there is one thing that you'll make sure is true: that you're coachable. Here are Rebecca Morgan's insights on this process.

Are You Coachable?
by Rebecca Morgan CSP, CMC

I do a lot of 1-on-1 executive and entrepreneurial coaching. Which means I have a lot of pre-engagement conversations with people who would like to create bigger results and think coaching could help.

But some aren't coachable—yet they don't know it.

Why do I say this?

The people with whom I enter a successful coaching relationship have several things in common that is missing in those with whom I don't begin a relationship.

The ones who are good coaching clients are:

- **Open to new ideas.** They don't immediately say, "That won't work for me." Not that I always have a perfect solution for them. But coachable people are more apt to say, "Help me through where I'm stuck thinking this won't work." Or "I'm having a hard time seeing how that would work given my restrictions. Tell me more." Or "I understand your idea, but I'd like to brainstorm some modifications to it."

- **Focused in the conversation.** They may go on brief tangents, but they know they're going there to make a point soon. They may even say, "This will sound tangential, but I'll bring it back." Those who aren't good coaching clients go off on long digressions and get irritated when I try to bring it back to the topic.
- **Respectful of our time together.** They know every minute we have is precious and they come prepared with an agenda based on the priorities they want to cover. They don't dilly dally.
- **Not argumentative.** When they disagree they do so respectfully, as I work to do.
- **Focused on implementation.** They use me as a sounding board to help them move through what's stopping them and are committed to the execution plan we co-create. They know excuses keep them stuck so they make regular progress on the tasks set out to achieve what they want.
- **Honest with themselves and with me.** If they know they are procrastinating, they say so, not try to hide it.
- **Savvy in understanding that the coach isn't going to do their work for them.**
- **Truly want help,** not to make it seem that they don't really need help.
- **Willing to hear direct, respectful feedback,** not be told that something they've produced is good when it isn't.
- **Don't go on and on about minutia** that isn't relevant to the issue at hand. They are paying me

for my perspective, insights, questions and advice and they know to get value they have to allow me to share what I think would be useful to them.
- **Able to know when they are being too needy.** Coaches usually have agreements that outline how often there will be communication. While there can be emergencies or extenuating circumstances, it's important that both parties acknowledge when there's more contact—or less—than what's been contracted.

Rebecca L. Morgan, CSP, CMC, specializes in creating innovative solutions for customer service challenges. She's appeared on *60 Minutes, Oprah, the Wall Street Journal, National Public Radio* and *USA Today*. Rebecca is the bestselling author of 25 books, including *Calming Upset Customers* and Professional *Selling*. She is an exemplary resource who partners with you to accomplish high ROI on your strategic customer service projects. For information on her services, books, and resources, or for permission to repost or reprint this article, contact her at
408/998-7977, Rebecca@RebeccaMorgan.com,
http://www.RebeccaMorgan.com decided

* * * * * * *

A number of people lament that the Law of Attraction has not given them the big breakthrough. The truth is: there are certain elements that are holding the person back. I'm pleased to share with you Morgana Rae's insights in how you can break down internal barriers to the Big, Positive Transformation for your life.

How I Hit My FIRST 6-Figure Year
by Morgana Rae

Would you like to hear how I had my **FIRST 6-figure year?**

(And have been multiplying that ever since?)

This is a story I've shared with my coaching clients, but I don't think I've ever shared it publicly.

This happened nearly ten years ago. It really started with a shift of consciousness.

And then it got really messy. Totally not what I expected.

I had already slayed my money monster, and I had my Money Honey. My finances were stable. I was making a decent living, and I was aware that I was hitting a way-too-low ceiling of what was possible for me.

I made a decision, as I was designing my new lesson for the year, (those of you who have done the Renewal Ritual in my *Financial Alchemy* workbook on Amazon know what I'm talking about) that I was going to **"take off the limits of what I believed possible for myself."**

Boy did that change things for me! Because as soon as I took off the limits of what I believed possible for myself, **I took off the limits on what I'd been investing in my business.** I started spending money like someone who believed she was going to make 6-figures that year.

I bought all the classes, programs, and coaches I had been too cautious to buy in the past. I spent more than I ever had before. Without seeing my income rise.

It was like a bad joke. Not at all what I imagined when I set the intention to "remove limits."

By the time August came around, that year, **my bank account was at ZERO.** I swore to myself I wouldn't hire another coach.

But instead I charged another $8,000 to my credit card, transferred the balance to a 2.99% card, and flew across the country for a 2-day seminar on something I believed I needed to learn.

Because I believed in myself enough to invest with money I didn't have yet.

The teacher was awful. I don't recommend him. But someone IN the class with me made a suggestion* while we shared a cab ride back to the airport. I took her advice. And here's what happened:

I had my first $20,000 month when I got home.

Followed by my first $30,000 month.

Followed by my first $50,000 month.

I made over $100,000 in under 90 days! After never having reached that before in a 12 month period. **I was a bigger person, and I could never go back to playing small.**

I learned some golden lessons that still work for me today. Here are my **4 BIG TAKEAWAYS:**

1) If you want to succeed, you must make decisions from the perspective of your successful future-self.

Those decisions will always be more expansive and courageous than decisions based on fear and lack of confidence.

2) Don't let your circumstances make your decisions.

I invested in myself even when I had debt. Debt is temporary. Never wait until such-and-such happens to take action. That thing you're waiting for is waiting for YOU to step up. The clients and the money always come AFTER you act like the person you want to be.

3) My success doesn't depend on my coaches.

I'm going to get really honest and personal here. I've

hired some truly terrible coaches. And I've made that "mistake" more than once. 'Cause I tend to see the best in everybody, and I assume other people share my values. So I paid tens of thousands of dollars for programs and promises they never delivered. Once I paid them I discovered I knew more than they did, made more money than they did, and had better relationships than they did.

I never asked for a refund. (I probably should have.) I always felt this is my business, so it's my responsibility to make sure I grow and get something I need from the experience.

Often the real value was the other people I met in the group.

Or it was seeing exactly what NOT to do in my own business.

Or simply the act of believing in myself enough to invest at such a high level.

And I always multiplied my income and my happiness anyway.

4) Be the kind of coach/service provider YOU would want to have.

When your competitors are under-delivering, maybe even bringing down your industry, **this is an *opportunity* to be the solution!** You may not see the rewards overnight, but if you keep plugging away, respecting yourself and your clients, and delivering superior service and results, it WILL catch up to you. And your success will last!

It ALWAYS comes down to finding opportunities, not excuses. No matter what.

The clients, the money, the relationships come AFTER you say yes to yourself.

Because that's how life works.

Namaste.

– *Morgana Rae*

* The whole time I was in the class, I was getting emails from clients who were having breakthroughs. In fact one of my clients hit his first million while I was at the seminar, and I read his email out loud to the class. The advice my seminar friend gave me was that, given my client results were so dramatic, I shouldn't charge less than $1,500. So I went home, raised my price from $375 to $1,500, and immediately picked up 14 or 15 (It's so long ago I don't remember) new clients at the higher price. And 20 people hired me the next month. And so on. FYI... MORE people wanted to hire me as soon as I charged more.

Morgana Rae is an internationally acclaimed life coach, author, and professional speaker, and is regarded to be the world's top relationship with money coach. Morgana's groundbreaking program for attracting wealth has featured her in *Personal Excellence Magazine, Entrepreneur Magazine,* United Press International and The Wall Street Journal online. Morgana is the author of *Financial Alchemy: Twelve Months of Magic and Manifestation,* and she is a contributing author to the bestselling book *Inspiration to Realization,* ranked a "must read" by *Entrepreneur Magazine.* Morgana's *Financial Alchemy* books, CDs, magazine articles, and classes have impacted the lives of thousands of people worldwide. Morgana writes, speaks, and coaches from a desire to empower idealistic entrepreneurs, coaches, authors and artists to have a big impact in the world...and to heal the rift between heart, spirit, and money.

To Learn More Visit: www.abundanceandprosperity.com & www.morganaraemedia.com

BOOK TWO:
THE LAW OF CREATION –
WAKE UP YOUR SPIRT TO PROSPERITY

In this section you will learn Seven Powerful Steps to create the life you really want, including an abundance of time and money, spiritual fulfillment and loving relationships.

Ever feel like you're in a financial rut? This section will shine the light on your natural brilliance. Your natural brilliance is like diamonds just waiting to sparkle when you shine a light on them. Your natural brilliance will light your way out of your financial rut.

The difficulties related to climbing out of a financial rut came up recently. My client Stephanie said, "I'm afraid that the higher I go, the further I have to fall."

"We'll find a way to bring your safety net up with you," I replied. I helped her explore alternatives and uncover her hidden talents. As a success coach, I help clients and audiences stretch and nurture their spirits during the process. I can do the same for you.

What makes this book different from others is that I combine both the spiritual and practical approaches to wealth. As a faculty instructor of Comparative Religion (over 12 years), I guide my college students to experience the beauty and power of spiritual paths.

I then provide business strategies from my roles as America's Communication Coach and "The Personal Branding Instructor" (as reported by *The San Francisco Examiner*). I guide my clients to take action to gain more money, do well in business, and expand feelings of fulfillment. You will learn secrets I have used and the strategies of 18 people—millionaires and billionaires.

This book incorporates spiritual and practical methods to increase wealth. As you learn these methods, you condition yourself to be at your best when it really counts.

In a later section, I will share with you the powerful process of Personaltainment™ Branding, a new level of branding I created.

Through this strategy my clients increase their customer base more quickly and also enjoy the process.

You can feel inner peace while you experience the ups and downs necessary to increase your personal wealth and fulfillment.

Further along, you will learn practical methods of the Momentum Action Plan™ (MAP), also known as the 9-Minute Miracle Breakthrough. Use this process once a week or at the beginning of your day to target and do the best actions to improve your life. Learn to add zest to your moment-to-moment experiences. You will also learn to use leverage, which is to gain the maximum benefits from the least efforts.

Later in Book Two, you will learn how to deepen and warm up your relationships because, as researchers have shown, quality relationships are the basis for great business success and personal fulfillment. You will also learn the 30 Secrets of Humor to bring warmth and laughter to your relationships. Mark Burnett (creator of the TV shows *Survivor* and *The Apprentice* with Donald Trump) wrote, "Negotiation secret: If all else fails, make them laugh."

Enhancing relationships is a spiritual process. *Prosperity is about having more than money. It also includes financial freedom.*

Over the years my perspective has expanded as I enjoyed a number of adventures that required money, contacts and strategies. I am grateful for my experiences connected to prosperity including:

- Directing and producing feature films
- Traveling to various parts of the world
- Speaking at the National Association of Broadcasters Conference (the world's largest media conference) for six years in a row
- Teaching as a guest instructor at Stanford University
- Publishing my business books, music and novels
- Taking fun vacations with my romantic partner, her parents and my parents

From ordinary beginnings, I became the first college graduate in my family. I live with a lot of hope. In fact, a colleague asked me about my experiences of God; and I replied, "Times of delighted surprise."

Your path to enjoy more abundance begins now with this book. For more information concerning the topics in this book, you can reach me through my blog at

BeHeardandBeTrusted.com

The central idea of *Wake Up Your Spirit to Prosperity* is to get out of your own way.

To manifest what you truly want, you need to change your focus and wake up your spirit. Prosperity consciousness essentially means being awake.

Many of us experience great suffering concerning issues of money, prosperity and scarcity. Some don't realize that their financial details are part of their spiritual path. Spirituality includes the process of giving and receiving value. And prosperity is more than just money.

According to Dictionary.com, *prosperity* means "having success, flourishing, and having good fortune." It also states that prosperity is "an economic state of growth with rising profits and full employment." What we get from this definition is that prosperity is not just about money. Wake

Up Your Spirit to Prosperity talks about spiritual growth and full employment of your natural brilliance, that is, your gifts from Higher Power.

For our discussion, we will use the process: S.P. I.R.I.T.

S – Seek the Higher View
P – Program for abundance
I – Intuit to do it
R – Retreat from Reverse-Examples
I – Inspire hope and faith
T – Target the good of all

In the following sections we will dive into the methods outlined with S.P.I.R.I.T.

You can turn your life into a positive adventure that includes abundance. This book shows you how.

Let's continue ...

Seek the Higher View

By emphasizing a Higher View, I invite you to make a transition to seeing things from the viewpoint of your Higher Self. You can focus on your Higher Self or remain stuck in the Ego. The Ego is made of fear. When you are stuck in your Ego you feel small, vulnerable and fragile. A number of people, when stuck in their Ego, feel irritable and angry. Anger is fear twisted.

On the other hand, you can focus on your Higher Self, or what I usually refer to as your True Self.

Your True Self is that part of you that is strong, focused and filled with natural brilliance and courage.

To get unstuck from your Ego and seek the Higher View is to make a transition to your Higher Self as fast as possible. When you're seeing things from your Higher Self, you experience a form of peace, even when things around you are chaotic.

In Taoism the idea is to flow with the universe. The Tao (translated as "The Way") is often compared to a stream of flowing water. Imagine how much more effective you would be if you were like a canoe flowing with the stream instead of like a rock, complaining about the water striking you in the face.

That is, avoid complaining about your stagnation and lack of opportunity. Flow with opportunities that appear.

How can you flow with the universe? How can you wake up your spirit? Focus on this Question How can I serve?

Your focus point is better when it goes beyond your personal needs. You need to see how to make a contribution. Martin Luther King, Jr. said, "Everyone can be great because anyone can serve." Where do you serve? Right where you are.

One of my clients said in desperation, "Serve? I can't serve. I'm barely keeping my head above water now." I shared with her that to wake up her spirit to prosperity is to expand her perceptions. Focusing only on one's urgent, immediate needs is like wearing blinders to the possibilities of service and, as a dividend, expanding earnings. The Ego is stuck in fear and is a small focus area.

To help you look beyond the Ego and its small focus area, let's view the differences between the Higher Self and the Ego.

Two Aspects of Your Self	
Higher Self	**Ego**
Abundance	Scarcity
Expansive	Contracting, pain-avoiding, reactive
Creative	Cowering
How may I serve?	What's in it for me?
Serve where you are.	Wait for a purpose to come along
Faith	Doubt
Love-mode	Fear-mode

The elements (above) related to the Higher Self all relate to Prosperity Consciousness.

On the other hand, all of the elements (above) related to the Ego relate to Scarcity Consciousness.

Back to Prosperity Consciousness: To attract prosperity focus on being in "love-mode." The idea of the love-mode is to focus on being helpful, which is a Higher Self approach. Also, many of us turn to Higher Power (some say "Spirit" or "God") who can guide us.

How do we, stuck in the real world and dealing with our daily lives, stay in the Higher Self? We memorize phrases that shift the directions of our thoughts.

Memorize phrases to shift your thoughts in a positive direction. Here are examples:
- Be still and know that I am God. (The Bible)
- Minds debate. Hearts relate. (Ann Wilson Schaef)
- We must not allow any force to make us feel like we don't count. Maintain a sense of dignity and respect. (Martin Luther King, Jr.)
- You must be the change you wish to see in the

world. (Gandhi)
- Do not lay on any soul a load which you would not wish to be laid upon yours. (Baha'i)
- If you want others to be happy, practice compassion. If you want to be happy, practice compassion. (The Dalai Lama)
- You cannot solve a problem on the same level in which it was created. (Albert Einstein)
- Let no come to you without leaving better. (Mother Teresa)
- Our fears must never hold us back from pursuing our hopes. (John F. Kennedy)

Another way to shift your thoughts and feelings is through music. I can change my thoughts by humming the tune and words of an empowering song. And, I recall the exuberant music of *Indiana Jones* or *Superman, the Movie*.

Shifting your thoughts and feelings is important related to fear. We do not want get stuck in fear because that might prevent us from taking appropriate action. If you feel a touch of fear, realize that this is just a beginning. Now it's time to step forward.

Intensify the Power of Words

Some paragraphs ago, I shared a secret with you—the power of music. Our target is to use the power of your subconscious mind. In an article in *U.S. News and World Report*, writer Marianne Szegedy-Maszak reported: "Cognitive neuroscientists [identify that] most of our decisions, actions, emotions, and behavior depends on the 95 percent of brain activity that goes beyond our conscious awareness." Realizing this fact, I have my clients associate music, body posture, and an image to words they want to memorize.

For example, Phil played the theme music of *Superman, the Movie* while repeating the words from one of my books:

"Courage is easier when I'm prepared." He stood up straight and strong as he held in mind an image of himself wearing a hero's cape. This combination of music, body posture, image and words helps Phil make decisions and take action when he is an empowered state of being.

I summarize this process with these words: *You must magnetize what you memorize.* Some magnets are empowered by a strong electrical current. Similarly, power-up your ability to shift to a Higher View by using a combination of words, music, body posture, and an image.

Principle

Shift to a Higher View. Shift the direction of your thoughts by using a combination of memorized phrases, music, body posture, and an image.

Author Anthony Robbins said, "Successful people ask better questions, and as a result, they get better answers." Along these lines, I am including a Leverage Question for each of these sections. Leverage is like using a stick and a small rock as the fulcrum to move a boulder. Through leverage you can support the flow of grand abundance in your life.

Here is our first Leverage Question.

Leverage Question

What ideas do you want to memorize (and repeat to yourself) so you can quickly shift the direction of your thinking? What music, image and body posture can you add to engage your real power?

Program for Abundance

Another definition of prosperity is "a state of being very lively and profitable." It's your choice: You can live in love-mode or fear-mode. To achieve the best results, program your mind for abundance, which comes from the love-mode.

We seek to override the scarcity programming that may have been *placed there by parents or relatives.*

What does scarcity sound like? "We can't afford it." Abundance includes empowering phrases.

Mindsets	
Scarcity	**Abundance**
We can't afford it.	How can we gain more money?
	How can we serve more people?

Train your mind to see the abundance in life. Here's an example—A friend invites you to an event that is too costly. The idea is to reply with something that empowers you. You can say: "My family's budget is going in a different direction at the moment." Remember that your subconscious mind is listening at all times. Train it with thoughts of abundance, rather than thoughts of scarcity.

Budgets are a useful part of life. Budgets help people plan for vacations; and feature films get made via budgets. Learn to let go of your fear of that word. Do some research and find out the numbers before making a decision. For example, one of my clients, an aspiring author, discovered that she can self-publish copies of her book for only $150 through the print-on-demand process. She moved toward abundance and accomplished her goal of publishing, without getting bogged down in fear. The idea is to take a step forward.

For example, the best-selling book *The Celestine Prophesy* was first self-published. Then a major publisher took notice, and subsequently, millions of copies were sold.

Find out the numbers, and you're one step closer to your dream.

It helps to drop "I can't afford it" from your speech pattern. "I can't afford it" puts you in a world of pain. Instead, put yourself into the world of possibility—a world of abundance.

One interviewer asked me: "The reality could be that someone really cannot afford it. What if the person really wants both things, and can only get one thing?" I responded by talking about a time, many years ago, when a friend and I were in a bookstore. I selected eight books but felt the need to put back seven. At the time my funds were needed for things like rent, food, and bus fare. But I wasn't disturbed because I knew that eventually I would have the money to get any book I wanted. However, my friend was upset. She didn't have the mindset that more prosperity was on the way.

One millionaire told me about a mindset that helped him. He had the phrase: "I'm a millionaire. The funds may not yet be in my bank account—but I'm a millionaire."

You need to program your thoughts and actions so that you support *the flow of abundance in your life.*

I encourage you to engage with the insights and methods throughout this book, particularly the questions at the end of each section. Becoming stronger is a process that requires you to take action.

When you are serious about opening the gate to a better flow of financial abundance, consider: A great idea is to make your work a prayer.

Mother Teresa said, "Prayer does not demand that we

interrupt our work, but that we continue working as if it were a prayer."

To increase abundance, move beyond patterns that limit your progress, like trading your time for money.

When you want to make a leap beyond your current level of abundance, you need to get out of the limiting pattern of trading your time for money.

My next example comes from someone I have learned from directly, C.J. Hayden. Her book *Get Clients Now* details a methodology for effectively gaining clients in a way that fosters ease in her reader's life. To guarantee continued sales of her book, C.J. created the Licensee Kit, a program by which personal coaches use her book and methodology for their clients. To use C.J.'s successful program, coaches must ask their clients to buy copies of Get Clients Now. At the time of this writing the Complete Package, Training, and Renewable License is priced at $795.

From C.J.'s example, we learn to move beyond trading time for money. As a personal coach C.J. can only make an hourly fee. But the magic happened when she made the shift to being the creator of a franchise!

The Power-3 Income Streams

We can learn from C.J. Hayden about the process of creating multiple streams of income. But the crucial detail is to avoid scattering your energy. I learned this when a millionaire told me: "I see a lot of activity, but I don't know how productive it is."

I brought this insight into my coaching work. Over the years, I have seen clients who *dabbled in many money-making activities* before they met me. In response, I invited my clients to improve efficiency and reduce the number of scattered activities they were involved in. I introduced them to The Power-3 Income Streams:

- *Income Stream 1: **Stability (your base).*** One of my clients is a teacher, which forms her base. She can take appropriate time to analyze her stream of income opportunities. She is neither desperate nor harried.
- *Income Stream 2: **Automatic.*** A number of my clients make money through the Internet—while they are sleeping.
- *Income Stream 3: **No ceiling.*** A number of my clients are creating books, audio programs, and inventions. They know that when something becomes a hit, there is no ceiling on the amount of money they can make.

When creating a product, it is helpful to hear about the trials successful people endured. It often takes more than one product to become successful. For example, Richard Carlson, author of the *Don't Sweat the Small Stuff* series, told me that *Don't Sweat the Small Stuff* was his tenth book.

Another example: The ThighMaster® (promoted by Susanne Somers), which earned $100 million, was the second item on an eight-item plan of inventions. Peter Bieler, the leader of the ThighMaster team, knew that out of eight products some would fail and some would work. The team was fortunate: After the first item failed (and they learned from the process), the second item was a hit. Peter Bieler knew there was no ceiling to their future abundance.

Using the Power-3 Income Streams (Stability, Automatic and No Ceiling) helps you to avoid scattering your energy-and working on too many income streams at once.

Program for Abundance by Asking for Help

Another way to program for abundance is to ask for

Higher Power's help. Best-selling authors Jack Canfield and Mark Victor Hansen (co-creators of the *Chicken Soup for the Soul* series) emphasize the power of asking. In their book *The Aladdin Factor* they describe hundreds of effective ways of asking for what you want.

Open the door to healing with the God Box

When you turn over your worries and cares to Higher Power, you open the door to healing. Write down what really troubles you and place it in a beautiful, small box — your God Box. Do not read the slip of paper ever again. As you place your paper in the box, recite a prayer like: "God, I turn this over to you. This is too big for me. I ask for Your help and healing so I feel better about this. I seek to do my part better. May this situation turn out for the good of all involved. Thank you. Amen."

Principle

Focus on abundance in every situation. Find ways to move beyond trading your time for money.

Leverage Question

How can I serve more effectively and keep abundance flowing?

[It helps to get a personal journal and answer the question posed at the end of each section. Take 20 seconds and write down your immediate thoughts. You'll gain more benefit from this process.]

Intuit to do it

When I talk about intuit to do it, I'm referring to a strategy that taps into your deepest powers. Intuit to do it means using your intuition to help gain energy, direction and the power to keep going until you complete something crucial to obtain abundance in your life.

"What if I'm intuition impaired?" asked a woman in one of my audiences.

"Perhaps, you're referring to the practice of not making space for your intuition," I responded. We all get feelings about things. We just need to acknowledge them and honor them. Dictionary.com defines intuition as "Immediate cognition … The act or faculty of knowing or sensing without the use of rational processes … An impression."

Sometimes we get a flash of insight or a gut feeling about something. For example, a woman seeking more customers for her barbershop realized she needed to reposition her business. She listened to her intuition which told her the best way to attract more male clients (her target customer) was to create a sports theme in her shop. She set up her barbershop like a sports bar with sporting events on the television set and sports-related magazines. Her business flourished, that is, prospered.

Researchers note that self-made millionaires follow through on their hunches. Also, a number of millionaires have said, "You only have to be right 51% of the time."

The important thing is to make space for your intuition.

I give speeches on the topic *Say YES to Yourself*. The idea is that you may need to say "no" to some things to create space so you can say "yes" to other things that focus on your top priorities.

I once gained 4 hours in 30 seconds. That is, I deleted four TV shows from my DVR (digital video recorder).

It's about making good choices. To make good choices we need to create *think-space*. When someone asks you to do something, give yourself time to think and, when it's appropriate, respond by saying: "I'll have to check my schedule when I get back to my desk. How about I call you this afternoon to see if I can fit that in?" This gives you the time and space to think about your decision to the offer.

So how do activate your intuition? First, think favorably about your intuition. Remember the times when you listened to your gut feelings and things turned out well. Second, make time for your intuition. Practitioners of Zen Buddhism and Hinduism set up time for daily meditation. Christians set time for daily prayer.

What if I don't have time for meditation?

One meditation guru was asked, "How long do you meditate?" He replied, "Three minutes a day." His point is that three minutes a day is better than planning to meditate 30 minutes a day—and you don't do it.

Will only three minutes do any good?

Yes. Zen Buddhists look for the sudden flash of insight known as satori, or intuitive illumination. A person can connect with Higher Power in just three minutes.

Carry a small memo pad in your pocket or purse so you can write down your insights. For example, some time ago I was riding a bicycle and, zap, I had an incredible idea for a novel or screenplay. This was a Wow! idea. I immediately wrote it down. If you are driving it might be best to pull your car over to the side of the street. If you write slowly, you can carry an audio recorder. Just be sure to capture the idea. The universe has just handed you a gift. Honor the abundance of the universe and write it down.

Mozart captured musical ideas that flowed into his mind. He wrote in a letter: "When I am, as it were, completely myself, entirely alone, and of good cheer—say traveling in a carriage, or walking after a good meal, or during the night when I cannot sleep: it is on such occasions that my ideas flow best and most abundantly. Whence and how they come, I know not; nor can I force them. Those ideas that please me I keep in my memory [by humming] them to myself."

Make plans and take action because the universe bestows great ideas to many, but only a few have the courage and persistence to take action and make their dreams come true.

Make space for your intuition. Be ready when opportunities arise. For example, there have been times late at night when my sweetheart asks me about some future event. During late hours when I feel tired my reflex is to say "no." So I tell her the truth and say, "If I answer now, I'll say no. So instead, let's talk about this tomorrow, okay?" This is how I make space for my intuition and subconscious mind, which will ponder the event while I sleep.

Principle
Intuit to do it.

Leverage Question
How can you effectively and kindly respond to people and create *think-space* for yourself?

Retreat from Reverse Examples

Some negative people say "That's too much trouble." Or, "That will never work." We can look at negative people as Reverse Examples. When you want a life of abundance and joy, you need to run—not walk—away from these people, the Reverse Examples.

I call negative people Reverse Examples because they are not standing still; they are actually going backwards. This is contrary to progress and does not support the flow of grand abundance.

I remember once walking to an appointment in

downtown San Francisco. Two men were arguing loudly. In my mind I said a prayer: "Blessings to you both." These two men, through their abusive language and tone, were Reverse Examples. They were not just standing still; they were causing damage to their relationship—and in effect they were going backwards.

When using the term Reverse Example to describe someone, it's important to realize that we are not judging that person, but defining a counterproductive action. No one has less value than any other person. The point here is that we need to value our intuition when selecting people to socialize with or think about. There are times when our intuition informs us that "I don't want to be like that person. She does not have the same goals I have. She doesn't want what I want. And she's not willing to pay the price I'm willing to pay to move forward."

Let's look at a healthy and spiritual way to interact with the people we call Reverse Examples. (And let's realize that a person can be both a good example in some area and a Reverse Example in another area.) People want closeness and competence. If you find yourself engaged in something that is creating space (a separation) and implying that the other person is not competent, STOP. Yes, stop. Even if you need to say, "Excuse me. I'll be right back. I need to go to the restroom."

When you return, identify something that you feel the other person is doing correctly. Also, identify your positive intention. For example, one evening, my sweetheart was watching television while I worked on a book—in another room. When I saw her after her programs, I felt uncomfortable. Instead of saying, "You're not spending enough time with me" which would put her on the defensive, I started with my intention and said gently: "I missed you." That created closeness.

When you want more abundance, watch out for the people who are focused on comfort first. These people don't take appropriate risks. Not taking appropriate risks can be a Reverse Example.

A Native American Elder (as quoted by Ann Wilson Schaef) said, "When the Creator gives you something, don't hesitate. Grab it." From this we realize that we must stretch to create a new phase of life that is different from all we have experienced thus far. To learn how to take appropriate risks, you need to feed your mind and spirit with examples of how people have accomplished the extraordinary. The process of successful and appropriate risk-taking is an important part of the journey to manifest wealth and a fulfilling life. And in this section, we will soon learn about risk-taking and more from selected Inspiring Examples: millionaires and billionaires.

The idea of retreat from Reverse Examples points to spiritual processes. People go on retreats to renew their spirits, minds and bodies. But you can have mini retreats during your normal day. These are moments that align with Psalm 46:10: "Be still and know I am God." Some scholars point out that this means: Relax a moment and remember that God is running the universe.

A mini retreat is a moment you take for yourself when you focus on a positive thought. When you do this you give yourself to Higher Power and offer up your stress. For example, when you walk to the restroom during a busy day at work, you can say a prayer in your mind—and have a mini retreat.

The idea of "Be still and know I am God" and taking a mini retreat ties in with something called the Activity-Recovery Pattern. Researchers have found that the most effective people do not work fast and constantly and without breaks. The most productive people use an Activity-Recovery Pattern that includes times of rest and recovery. For example, my morning often includes an intense period of writing. When I am done I get up from my computer or notepad and take time to exercise. My mind recovers while my body moves.

With my audiences, I emphasize *take breaks or be broken*. Pace yourself and use an Activity-Recovery Pattern.

Some people combine prayer and exercise. I know people who pray and walk on a treadmill for five minutes—three times a day for a daily total of 15 minutes. A landmark Harvard study noted that a mere 15 minutes a day for a total of one or two hours a week will improve a person's health. Those who do this have a 50% better chance to avoid a heart attack, and reduce the possibility of heart surgery. This is terrific news. In just 15 minutes you can combine exercise with prayer or meditation to achieve a healthy body and a healthy spirit.

People who procrastinate are Reverse Examples. On the other hand, people who enjoy abundance do not procrastinate. They take action. Here is a powerful tool I use everyday: The Morning 8. Every morning for eight minutes I take action on whatever issue is crucial for my success. I find it helps to take on these challenges in the morning, when my mind and body are still fresh.

The Morning 8 is when you do what you don't like to do first thing in the morning, when your mind and body are fresh and free from the stress of the coming day.

For example, people who are buried in clutter might devote eight minutes each day to clearing their desks. Over a year (that is, 5 days a week for 51 weeks), that would add up to 34 hours. Imagine how your life could be free of clutter when 34 hours or almost a full work-week was devoted to eliminating disorder.

Avoid Reverse Examples & Seek Out Inspiring Ones

Reverse Examples have quick, easy answers to many new situations: "Don't do it; you'll get hurt" or "The odds are against you getting what you want."

The important idea is to move away from Reverse Examples and their limited patterns of thought. Seek out Inspiring Examples, that is, those people who have done the extraordinary!

Let's learn from fourteen millionaires and four billionaires about their processes to create financial abundance:

1. **Oprah Winfrey:** "Though I'm grateful for the blessings of wealth, it hasn't changed who I am. My feet are still on the ground. I'm just wearing better shoes." She also said, "The key to realizing a dream is to focus not on success but on significance—and then even the small steps and little victories along your path will take on greater meaning …. For every one of us that succeeds, it's because there's somebody there to show you the way out. The light doesn't always necessarily have to be in your family; for me it was teachers and school …. My philosophy is that not only are you responsible for your life, but doing the best at this moment puts you in the best place for the next moment …. You get in life what you have the courage to ask for." She also said, "Always continue the climb. It is possible for you to do whatever you choose, if you first get to know who you are and are willing to work with a power that is greater than ourselves to do it."

2. **Bill Gates:** "I think it's fair to say that personal computers have become the most empowering tool we've ever created. They're tools of communication, they're tools

of creativity, and they can be shaped by their user." He also said, "It's a lot easier to connect to the story of the one person or the five people .... I know [that] there's 3 million kids every year dying of things that are completely preventable with the technology we have today." And he said, "Your most unhappy customers are your greatest source of learning."

3. **Donald Trump:** "What separates the winners from the losers is how a person reacts to each new twist of fate." He also said, "Find the right person, and second, monitor his or her progress .... Only a great contractor can make ten parties happy .... Never accept a contractor's first bid .... Never, ever accept a first offer .... It's moronic to be too proud to save money .... It is important to let people know about your accomplishments .... The best way to impress people is through results .... It doesn't matter whether the success is a small one or a big one—you have to start somewhere and build on it."

4. **Mark Victor Hansen** (co-creator of the *Chicken Soup for the Soul* series): "You control your future, your destiny. What you think about comes about. By recording your dreams and goals on paper, you set in motion the process of becoming the person you most want to be. Put your future in good hands—your own."

5. **Jack Canfield** (co-creator of the *Chicken Soup for the Soul* series): "My life purpose is to inspire and empower people to live their highest vision in a context of love and joy." He also said, "You only have control of three things in your life—the thoughts you think, the images you visualize and the actions you take [your behavior] .... You cannot improve your life, your relationships, your game or your performance without feedback .... Slow down and pay attention."

6. **Marty Rodriguez** (Century 21's top real estate agent): "Many people become our friends and like to hang around here .... Clients bring their friends .... One time my husband asked, 'Why do you do these things? You don't have to do these things.' I said, 'That's what makes me different.' "

7. **Anthony Robbins** (top motivational speaker and author): "A real decision is measured by the fact that you've taken a new action. If there's no action, you haven't truly decided." He also said, "One reason so few of us achieve what we truly want is that we never direct our focus; we never concentrate our power. Most people dabble their way through life, never deciding to master anything in particular." Also, "The only limit to your impact is your imagination and commitment."

8. **Liz Claiborne** (founder of Liz Claiborne, Inc. who directed the company's designers): "[When I started the company] the goal was to clothe the working American woman. I was working myself, I wanted to look good, and I didn't think you should have to spend a fortune to do it .... I'm a great believer in fit, in comfort, in color. And I listened to the customer. I went on the selling floor as a saleswoman, went into the fitting room, heard what they liked and didn't like."

9. **Brian Tracy** (author of numerous bestselling self help books): "I've found that luck is quite predictable. If you want more luck, take more chances. Be more active. Show up more often." He also said, "Successful people are always looking for opportunities to help others. Unsuccessful people are always asking, 'What's in it for me?'" He said, "The more you seek security, the less of it you have. But the more you seek opportunity, the more likely it is that you will achieve the security that you desire." Also, "All successful men and women are big dreamers. They imagine what their

future could be, ideal in every respect, and then they work every day toward their distant vision, that goal or purpose."

10. **Warren Buffett** (listed by *Forbes* magazine as the third richest man in the world): "I only buy what I understand." He also said, "It's better to hang out with people better than you. Pick out associates whose behavior is better than yours, and you'll drift in that direction."

11. **Suze Orman** (#1 *New York Times* best-selling author, known as "America's most trusted personal finance expert"): "People first, then money, then things … To choose [to be] rich is to make every penny count, every dollar count, every financial choice count." Also, "In all realms of life it takes courage to stretch your limits, express your power, and fulfill your potential … it's no different in the financial realm." She wrote, "Truth Creates Money, Lies Destroy it."

12. **Robert G. Allen** (best-selling author): "Don't let the opinions of the average man sway you. Dream, and he thinks you're crazy. Succeed, and he thinks you're lucky. Acquire wealth, and he thinks you're greedy. Pay no attention. He simply doesn't understand." He also said, "When you're doing what you love to do, the money comes naturally. Maybe not at first, but eventually … if you stick with it. Do you think Bob Hope started out with a goal, 'I want to become a millionaire by making people laugh, then I'll retire to do what I want'? I doubt it. He just did what he did best. And the money came."

13. **T. Harv Eker** (best-selling author of *Secrets of the Millionaire Mind*): "Rich people associate with positive, successful people. Poor people associate with negative or unsuccessful people."

14. **George Lucas:** "If you want to be successful … perseverance is one of the key qualities. It's very important that you find something that you care about, that you have a

deep passion for, because you're going to have to devote a lot of your life to it ... You're not going to get anywhere without working extremely hard ... years and years of very, very difficult struggle through the whole process of achieving anything ... The secret is not to give up hope. It's very hard not to because if you're really doing something worthwhile I think you will be pushed to the brink of hopelessness before you come through the other side. You just have to hang in through that."

15. **Steven Spielberg:** "A good director knows when to say 'yes.' ... The public has an appetite for anything about imagination ... I've found some kind of new color that I never splashed against the canvas before .... I don't need to prove anything to anyone. I don't need to prove anything to myself. I just need to stay interested."

16. **Harvey Mackay** (bestselling author of *Swim with the Sharks without Being Eaten Alive*): "What I'll be doing a year from now [is] undoubtedly based on contacts I made today."

17. **Mary Kay Ash**, founder of Mary Kay Cosmetics (with $2 billion in sales): "When I meet someone, I imagine her wearing an invisible sign that says, 'Make me feel important! ... This is one of the most important lessons in dealing with people I have ever learned." Also, "I believe each of us has God-given talents within us waiting to be brought into fruition." She wrote, "It was not extensive market surveys or demographic studies that created the pink Cadillac [her way to motivate consultants to excel], just [my] pure and simple woman's intuition." She noted: "The desire for recognition is a powerful motivator. Anyone who has attended a Mary Kay Seminar knows we recognize our people's achievement with beautiful gifts and tons of verbal appreciation. Exciting prizes are significant symbols of esteem: I believe both words and things are important." Finally, she said at a Mary

Kay Seminar: "Are you ready for the most exciting moment of your life?"

18. **Walt Disney:** "We are not trying to entertain the critics. I'll take my chances with the public." Also, "Disneyland is a work of love. We didn't go into Disneyland just with the idea of making money." "Build the castle first [so the construction crew knows the magic we're making]." He said, "You don't work for a dollar—you work to create and have fun." He noted, "Everyone has been remarkably influenced by a book." Also, "If we didn't have deadlines, we'd stagnate ... [To juggle so many things,] I'm always close to projects when we're chewing over the basic idea. Once the pattern is set ... I let the staff take over, and I go on to other things .... I have always had men working for me whose skills were greater than my own. I am an idea man .... Courage is the main quality of leadership ... usually it implies some risk—especially in new undertakings ... It is good to have a failure while you're young because it teaches you so much ... it makes you aware that such a thing can happen to anybody, and once you've lived through the worst, you're never quite as vulnerable afterward." Walt concluded, "I hope to stay young enough in spirit to never fear failure."

Wow! There are many useful strategies and wisdom condensed in what you have just read.

By the way, my life purpose is: *I help people experience enthusiasm, love and wisdom to fulfill big dreams.* And I am grateful to be working with you. Here is an important point: You can listen to the wisdom of millionaires and billionaire then go out and make new and powerful connections. In the next section we will see how I pulled together wisdom from effective people as I formulated Personaltainment™

Branding.

Principle
Retreat from Reverse Examples. Pay attention to what you need to learn and where you want to be.

Leverage Questions
Who and what are the Reverse Examples in your life? How can you get away from them or reduce your exposure time to them? Which people (who have already achieved what you want to do) can you focus on as Inspiring Examples? How can you use an Activity-Recovery Pattern?

Personaltainment Branding
Your Spiritual Path to Wealth

As I mentioned in the previous section, you can listen to the wisdom of millionaires and billionaires to learn to make new and powerful connections. That's how I formulated Personaltainment™ Branding. Personaltainment Branding can help you do well on the job—in a job interview, sales presentation or in building your own business.

Through Personaltainment Branding, I help my clients gain customers faster—with ease and feelings of personal fulfillment.

Personaltainment Branding is connecting with your prospective customers so they will know you and trust you quickly—and purchase what you offer.

For those of you who do not have external customers, you can still benefit from using the techniques in this chapter. Use these techniques with your supervisor and co-workers, who function like your internal customers. You still need to provide services for them, and you still need to keep them happy.

Let's continue to discuss branding. The standard form of branding is the association of a brand with an idea, like Volvo and safety. Similarly, Disney is associated with family entertainment—and theme parks.

Then there is personal branding (which we will cover in more depth in a later section of this book). Here is an example of a personal brand: Tom Marcoux, America's Communication Coach.

The central idea of a personal brand is to answer the question

"What are you best known for?" For example, I use the phrase "When you need to make them go 'Wow!'" to illustrate how I help clients impress audiences, prospective customers and others.

I have designed Personaltainment Branding as a step up from personal branding. That is, when you use Personaltainment Branding, you have an advantage over conventional personal branding. The central idea of Personaltainment Branding is for you to create for your prospective customer an experience that is:

- Personalized
- Entertaining
- Connecting

I call this the PEC Triangle. Now I'll give you a specific example about "connecting."

My client Dr. JoAnn Dahlkoetter (bestselling author of *Your Performing Edge* at DrJoAnn.com) asked for my help on a press release during the 2006 Winter Olympic Games. As a coach to Olympic athletes, she wanted to be interviewed on numerous television and radio shows.

My first thought was that she needed to make her message connecting to ordinary viewers of TV and radio shows. The problem is that her clients, Olympians, are extraordinary people. How could she reach viewers? We decided to focus on what all people need: Skills to bounce back after a difficult struggle. I suggested that her press release include the following: "People must become skilled at bouncing back, whether it's crashing on ski slopes or crashing in a boardroom presentation," says Dr. JoAnn.

This was especially relevant because Dr. JoAnn had recently coached one of her Olympians to bounce back and regain confidence after a skiing accident that resulted in a concussion.

Finally, Dr. JoAnn's press release included this phrase:

"After Michelle Kwan's withdrawal and Jacobellis' fall, Dr. JoAnn Dahlkoetter can explain how people overcome fear and the strategies to recover quickly from failure."

Dr. JoAnn's press release secured interviews for her on NBC Television, Newsweek on Air/Associated Press Radio, KCBS Radio, Bloomberg on the Air in New York and many others.

You Can Use Personaltainment Branding at Work

These techniques only require a pen and sheet of paper—and the following effective questions.

Five Personaltainment Branding Questions
1. What about this is working for you? (personalized)
2. When did this become fun for you? (entertaining)
3. What's most important about this for you? (personalized)
4. In order for you to know that you have what you want, what has to happen? (connecting)
5. How can we make this work better for you? (connecting)

(Another version of Question 2 is: When could this

become fun for you?)

You can use these questions with co-workers, prospective customers and current customers.

How Is Personaltainment Branding Spiritual?

In this book we talk about *how may I serve?* Also, we note that Mother Teresa said, "Make your work a prayer." Many of us seek to find spiritual and uplifting ways to work. Fortunately, the Personaltainment Branding process serves the prospective customer in the following ways:

- Personalized means you are important to me.
- Entertaining is giving the customer an enjoyable experience.
- Connecting helps fill the customer's empty feeling of loneliness.

The Foundation of Personaltainment™ Branding

Now that you've had a taste of the process, let me describe how Personaltainment Branding first occurred to me. I listened to certain ideas from Bill Gates: "I think it's fair to say that personal computers have become the most empowering tool we've ever created. They're tools of communication, they're tools of creativity, and they can be shaped by their user."

I then recalled Anthony Robbins' idea: "We aren't in an information age, we are in an entertainment age." Also, from Johnny Carson: "People will pay more to be entertained than to be educated."

I noticed the difference between Baskin-Robbins ice cream shops and Cold Stone Creamery. Baskin-Robins provides a selection of 31 Flavors. On the other hand, Cold Stone Creamery sells ice cream and the choice of add-ins, like chocolate syrup or fudge brownies. Cold Stone Creamery also provides helpful suggestions about add-ins that go together. One combination is called Cherry Cake Double Take®. The Cold Stone Creamery process is thus personalized.

With the iPod and iTunes, music is personalized. At the time of this writing, the online iTunes Music Store has sold more than 10 billion copies of songs.

You can make a lot of money by providing your service in a way that allows the customer to *personalize how he or she uses the service.*

We do best to move forward and let go of dinosaur thinking. Stubborn individuals who refuse to do so will become as extinct as the dinosaur! Look for ways to get ahead of the curve. Keep current by perusing the Internet (including blogs) to see what is in the global consciousness.

Now is the time of Personaltainment™—the time when prospective customers respond best to gestures that are personalized, entertaining and connecting.

Now we'll look at how Amazon.com customers have experiences that match the Personaltainment Branding process.

Example 1: A quick analysis of Amazon.com:

Personalized: Customers are given personalized recommendations based on past purchases and items placed in personal wish lists.

Entertaining: The customer's curiosity and feelings related to suspense are aroused so that she or he returns regularly to see what new items are being recommended.

Connecting: The customer can see lists like Listmania and So You Want To … that are written by other customers who share an interest. This might include advice, books and DVDs to help someone do something like write a book. This strategy develops the feeling of community.

Example 2: A quick analysis of Nightingale-Conant.com (a website for personal development):

Personalized: The prospective customer (or prospect) types answers about personal characteristics, into a form and gets a computer-designed Personal Mission Statement.

Entertaining: Receiving the Personal Mission Statement is fun, like seeing a daily horoscope at MSN.com.

Connecting: Having received something (the Personal Mission Statement), the prospect feels a connection to Nightingale-Conant. The prospect will then browse the site to find educational programs that can assist in the realization of her or his dream.

Increase Your Abundance Using Personaltainment Branding

I created a form (visible in the next pages) to help a business owner or salesperson design a prospective customer's experience. With Personaltainment Branding, the idea is to make them go "Wow!"

Personaltainment™ Branding
Make them go "Wow!"

Example of website strategies

1. Personalized

See: Include a questionnaire to find out what energizes the prospective customer about his or her work.

Hear: Not applicable.

Touch: The prospective customer types in his or her responses to the questionnaire.

2. Entertaining

See: Prospect receives the computerized response to the

questionnaire—which is like getting a horoscope: ("Oh, look at what it says!")

Hear: Include an audio link of the business owner praising the prospect for filling out the questionnaire. Music is played in the background.

Touch: The prospective customer types in her or his responses to questionnaire.

3. Connecting

See: Set up the questionnaire's response to include the prospect's first name in different places.

Hear: Include an audio link with the business owner saying: "Congratulations on devoting the time to fill out the form and get answers. We have found that highly motivated and effective people like you are the ones who complete the form and participate in the process. Well done. Now we will … "

Touch: Use music. Some music actually gives people a physical, positive response—a tingle along the spine, for example.

* * * * * *

Personaltainment Branding
Make them go "Wow!"

Website strategies

1. Personalized
See:

Hear:

Touch:

2. Entertaining
See:

Hear:

Touch:

3. Connecting
See:

Hear:

Touch:

(c) Tom Marcoux   BeHeardandBeTrusted.com

Personaltainment Branding Does Not Require a Fancy Website ...
When you use the Five Personaltainment Branding Questions, you can devise a compelling experience for the prospective customer in any way you interact with the

person—in-person, via email, and on the telephone. Again, here are the questions.

Five Personaltainment Branding Questions
1. What about this is working for you? (personalized)
2. When did this become fun for you? (entertaining)
3. What's most important about this for you? (personalized)
4. In order for you to know that you have what you want, what has to happen? (connecting)
5. How can we make this work better for you? (connecting)

For example, you are connecting when you ask someone, "What's most important to you about this?" The response you receive will give a clue as to how you can personalize your next comment and what you can offer that person.

Here's your opportunity to fill in a blank form to apply these ideas to your own work or service to customers. Personaltainment Branding is a helpful way to distinguish yourself in the marketplace. It is a powerful tool to give the prospective customer a Wow! experience that leads to becoming your customer faster. Personaltainment Branding also builds trust quickly. Everyone wins!

Furthermore, Personaltainment Branding is part of your spiritual path to wealth. It helps you wake up your spirit to prosperity. It helps you see things in a new light. It will give you a new perspective on how to serve people in the way they prefer to be served: personalized, entertaining and connecting.

Principle

To serve effectively, give the customer a Personaltainment Branding experience that is personalized, entertaining and connecting.

Leverage Question

Review the Personaltainment Branding process. How can you apply it to your work and use it to inspire prospective customers?

Inspire Hope and Faith

To experience a Higher-Self-mode of living, it is important to focus on hope and faith. Rabbi Harold Kushner wrote a book called *When All You've Ever Wanted Isn't Enough.* That's a powerful title. The truth is that many times what we thought we wanted is truly not enough. For example, a huge amount of money is not enough to bring inner peace. Johnny Carson said, "The only thing money gives you is the freedom of not worrying about money."

Hope and faith bring inner peace

At Dictionary.com, faith is defined as "a confident belief in the truth, value, or trustworthiness of a person, idea, or thing" and "a set of principles or beliefs."

So what do you believe? When you want more abundance, consider these beliefs:

- I learn from all experiences.
- Higher Power has a plan for me. Higher Power is watching over me.
- I am safe.
- I am worthy.
- Money is a tool I use well for the benefit of all.
- I easily gain money because I lovingly serve others in effective ways that attract money.
- To those God has given much, God enjoys their enjoyment.

This last comment, "God enjoys their enjoyment," relates

to Psalm 118:24: "This is the day the Lord has made; let us rejoice and be glad in it." It is appropriate and honorable to be grateful and rejoice. And rejoice means to feel happiness or joy—and to express great joy.

To express appreciation and joy is respectful of Higher Power. Be a fountain of positive energy, and your energy will bless the people around you.

Note that suffering is not the only road to wisdom. Misery not only loves company; misery creates company.

When you are feeling down, you can use a process to switch the direction of your thoughts: Take out a piece of paper (or just think this through in your mind) and write "I am grateful for ..." Then complete the sentence with ten examples. Instantly, your perception is expanded.

In my Comparative Religion college classes, I talk about healthy humility.

Healthy humility is acknowledging that *our ego often clouds our perception*, and we often do not know what supports our highest good.

Since we often do not know what supports our highest good, an effective prayer includes an ending of "this situation or better." My client Sandra wants a particular agent to represent her books, but then she remembers to add to her prayer: "this agent or an agent that would be a better match for me and my material."

We need to be humble. We don't see the whole picture in a given moment. Author Tama J. Kieves wrote: "The path of inspiration defies navigation. We arrive by way of revelation."

We live in hope and faith. And we live to witness revelations in our lives. Our search for personal truth goes like this: We receive a bit of guidance. We climb to a peak. We see more. Then we start up to a higher peak.

Joe Karbo, author of *The Lazy Man's Way to Riches*, took such a journey. Joe was deeply in debt. He consulted four lawyers and a judge and learned the extent of the law and how to interact with creditors to gain agreement to reasonable payment plans. He wrote a book based on his experiences that sold 100,000 copies, which significantly reduced his debt.

To create abundance, many people learn to solve a problem— and then teach others how to solve that problem.

To increase abundance, focus on hope. Mary Kay Ash, founder of Mary Kay Cosmetics (with $2 billion in annual sales), said, "Give yourself something to work toward— constantly." Write down what you are looking forward to. For example, one goal can be to earn extra money for a family vacation.

Also, when you design a product or service, have it serve people's hopes. Author Peter Nivio Zarlenga said, "In our factory, we make lipstick. In our advertising, we sell hope."

The important point to remember is that we can choose beliefs that support our path of abundance. We can believe that we have natural abilities and that Higher Power will help us to serve many people, and as a dividend, earn financial freedom.

Principle

Choose beliefs that build up your spirit and personal energy.

Leverage Question

Which of your beliefs support your path toward abundance?

Target the Good of All

One definition of prosperity is tending to favor or bring good luck. When you target the good for all involved, you align with the goodness of the universe. And this helps you attract good luck.

Let's begin by talking about forgiveness. In his book *Forgive For Good*, Dr. Fred Luskin talks about forgiveness as the process by which one ends a personal cycle of blame and suffering. We learn to become the hero of our own story instead of being a victim. One of my clients said, "My brother always beat me up when I was young." Imagine the power that emerges with the following substitution: "This is when I learned to value protecting myself. I asked my parents for karate lessons."

Consider this belief:

I can use everything to help me grow and serve more effectively.

When you focus on this belief, you can support a grand flow of abundance in your life. Learn to forgive—to free up your energy and create more abundance.

This section is about targeting the good of all. By all, I mean include yourself, your family, friends and your Higher Power.

Targeting the good of all is really about forgiveness, which is defined here as "seeing the big picture." The big picture is a more helpful definition of the word forgiveness than its more traditional meaning—pardon, a word that locks us into seeing a guilty person only as one who avoids punishment.

On the other hand, viewing forgiveness as the big picture allows us to go through the process of letting go of our painful feelings. For example, my client Marina received a huge disappointment. For months she helped her friend

Janet organize a conference. Marina assumed she would be rewarded with an opportunity to give a presentation at the event. Marina's speaking business was just starting, and she really needed a break. Marina had expressed to Janet her desire to give a speech.

At the last minute Marina discovered that she was not included on the conference agenda. It broke her heart. How could her friend Janet be so unfair and cruel?

I guided Marina through the Big Picture Forgiveness Process. Using the four-step process, Marina began by acknowledging her personal truth, which was that she felt deeply hurt. She overcame her disappointment by expanding her perspective.

The Big Picture Forgiveness Process

Step One: Acknowledge the pain. Marina said, "I'm really disappointed and hurt that Janet didn't give me the opportunity to serve her audience—especially after the help I gave her with the conference preparation."

Step Two: Take care of yourself. Marina treated herself with warm baths, relaxing music and time to write in her journal. She also processed her feelings as we talked through the situation.

Step Three: Examine the situation from the perspective of a metaphorical helicopter—to gain objectivity. In time, Marina was able to say, "Janet didn't include me on her list because she was only including speakers who already had a long list of fans. Janet was only focused on making her conference a success. I can understand that. But I still feel that she could have included me in some way. Since it was a spiritual conference, perhaps I could have led the prayer at dinner time."

Step Four: Become the hero of your own story. Marina

eventually said, "When Janet didn't include me in the conference, it became a warning sign that I need to change my perspective. I need to have faith that God will provide me with other opportunities. Also, I need to step up my participation. I need to intensify my focus. I really want to devote more time to marketing my own speaking career. I can't control what others do, but I can make better choices for myself."

Months later Marina still talks to Janet on the telephone from time to time. Marina's healthy approach to forgiveness has saved a friendship—and perhaps opened the door for her friendship with Janet to deepen over time. The good news is Marina is now free of her painful feelings. Her time and energy have been set free, too.

Within the word "forgiveness" are the letters that spell the word "free."

The Good of All Means Everyone Profits from a Situation

We start enjoying life to the fullest when we have learned to let go of hesitation around the word *profit*. Dictionary.com defines profit as "an advantageous gain or return; benefit." When you put service and Higher Power first, you can create profit in a holistic manner.

Author Harold Kushner wrote: "Our souls are not hungry for fame, comfort, wealth, or power ... Our souls are hungry for meaning."

To unlock the floodgates of abundance, we use this question:

How can you expand how you serve, in ways that are profitable and result in the dividend of abundance?

One speaker said, "Marriage is a place where you go to give—not just go to get." Find out how you can expand your contribution to the people in your life. And don't be shy about looking for profitable ways to accomplish your goals. For example, years ago, when working in a retail environment, I was trained to ask, "So what brings you into the store today?" I learned to say it in a friendly way. However, I would not be encouraging the customer to buy something if I approached her by only saying "How are you today?" I would not be serving both the person and the store.

You can make the interaction profitable for the person and for the store.

To target the good of all is to focus on how we conduct our daily lives. When I was in Japan, I witnessed a festival (known as matsuri) that is part of the indigenous religion Shinto. Shinto includes affirmations for family, tradition, reverence toward nature, physical cleanliness and festivals. The idea is, you can uplift your life when you affirm the valuable parts of it. Festivals, celebrations and rituals of worship that honor the Divine are helpful.

Author Sue Patton Thoele wrote: "Soothe your soul with ritual." Rituals keep spirituality in mind. Rituals remind people they are in a relationship with the Divine, and that relationship requires effort and time.

My client Mary celebrates her gratitude for her writing talent with a ritual, her annual "Joy in Writing Day." She purchases a book (she loves books), and she writes something for fun.

Rituals can be simple, brief and meaningful:

At every meal my sweetheart and I hold hands and say together, "We're grateful. Thank you."

Principle
Target the good of all involved.

Leverage Question

How can you expand how you serve, in ways that are profitable

and result in the dividend of abundance?

* * *

We have discussed the process S.P.I.R.I.T. and have examined the principles and Leverage Questions that will inspire you to achieve and support a grand flow of abundance in your life.

S – Seek the Higher View
P – Program for abundance
I – Intuit to do it
R – Retreat from Reverse Examples
I – Inspire hope and faith
T – Target the good of all

I have presented Seven Secrets (to wake up your spirit to prosperity), that include:

- The six methods of S.P.I.R.I.T., plus ...
- The process to serve the customer effectively: a Personaltainment™ Branding experience that is personalized, entertaining and connecting.

Author David Kundtz wrote that "Spirituality is the meanings and values by which you live your life combined with, for believers, the way your experience the divine. The combination of God, meanings and values is spirituality."

Walt Disney's brother and partner, Roy O. Disney, said, "Decision-making is easy if your values are clear."

You have the power to choose your beliefs and choose how you live on a daily basis. You can choose to focus on scarcity or abundance. You can remind yourself with "I am grateful for ... "

As I mentioned earlier, before I go to sleep each night I write in my Daily Journal of Victories and Blessings. A victory relates to an action I took—like exercising. A blessing is a gift—like talking on the telephone with an extended family member. I go to sleep feeling grateful for the blessings and adventures of each day.

I am grateful for the opportunity to connect with you through this book. I wish you a journey of love, abundance and blessings.

Let's continue with the next section ...

Make Money Through Your Natural Brilliance

In the previous section, you learned how to develop the mindset to expand your prosperity. So now the important thing is to progress forward. This section covers the 9-Minute Miracle Breakthrough. Once you learn the process, you can devote just nine minutes a day or even once a week to identifying what will really move you toward your dreams.

With the 9-Minute Miracle Breakthrough, I help my clients bring the process of prosperity expansion down to daily, individually tailored steps.

In this section, we will learn how to earn more money. Let's remember that money is a tool. For now, this affirmation is helpful: *Money is a tool that I use well for the benefit of all.* When you really feel this positive energy, you wake up your spirit to prosperity. We can see this process at work with Oprah Winfrey. Millions of people find her to be genuine and generous. And Oprah is the first African-American woman billionaire in U.S. history.

In this section you will create a Momentum Action Plan™

(MAP) as part of the 9-Minute Miracle Breakthrough. When you implement the Momentum Action Plan on a daily basis, you enjoy a new zest in your moment-to-moment experiences. You will also learn to use leverage, which means gaining the most benefit from the least effort.

My clients have found the 9-Minute Miracle Breakthrough to be more beneficial than standard time management and goal-setting practices. You will learn to use the power that is already inside you.

Science of the 9-Minute Miracle Breakthrough process

Over the years I developed the Science of Emotional Leverage™. The best way to describe leverage is with an image:

Imagine that you want to move a boulder. You place a small rock on the ground near the boulder. The small rock is your fulcrum. Then you use a big stick as your lever to move the boulder. With little effort you get big results. That's leverage.

Emotional Leverage is a strategy that utilizes your emotions to help you get big results with little effort. Emotional Leverage is how you free yourself for success.

Many people get frustrated and give up when they begin new methods or strategies—only to fall back to old habits. This disappointing situation results from a structural error in traditional training. When returning to old habits, these people are just waving around the proverbial stick and not using the key device, which is the fulcrum (or a little rock in our leverage metaphor).

The fulcrum represents merging with your True Self. Your True Self is the part of you that is naturally brilliant and courageous. On the other hand the False Self (also known as the Ego) is the part of you that is stuck in fear and feels caged. That's why we want to focus on your True Self—to help you free yourself from fear.

Make your True Self a bigger part of your daily life

Merging with your True Self is the process by which you consciously direct your thoughts away from fear and toward the perspective of abundance and spiritual growth. Eventually, like learning to ride a bicycle, you can maintain balance without conscious effort. The more you practice viewing life from your True Self, the more you experience merging with your True Self. Many people express that regular sessions of prayer or meditation help them experience inner peace. Such inner peace is a manifestation of the True Self.

This experience of inner peace is what martial arts masters refer to as being centered. Similarly, when Olympic athletes are "in the zone," they are focused. Creative people like writers talk about how words flow effortlessly. The point is that our emotions serve us to be productive when we merge with our True Self.

Your True Self saves you from procrastination.

Fear leads many of us to procrastinate. We seek to avoid pain. The good news is that the ten steps of the 9-Minute Miracle Breakthrough shift our attention away from pain. We get a new focus point. We do not shutdown because of pain. Instead, we begin with four questions to connect with the True Self.

At this point, pull out sheet of paper, notepad or a journal to write down questions and answers. By participating in the following process, you will form a roadmap to your best life. This roadmap is your Momentum Action Plan (MAP).

To be clear: When you go through the 9-Minute Miracle Breakthrough process, you end up with your Momentum Action

Plan.

In the Momentum Action Plan, you will be answering ten questions.

Momentum Action Plan (MAP)
Question 1: What do you want?

Choose any area in which you desire something. In just twenty seconds, write down whatever comes to mind. It can be a thing, a relationship, a new job, financial freedom, anything.

My clients have written:
- I want a new car.
- I want some new business clothes.
- I want my husband to treat me better.
- I want a career that satisfies my need for more prosperity, enriching friendships and exotic travel.
- I want to get a particular project done.

So write down what you want. Just a few words can be powerful.

This reminds me of a time when my parents and I were vacationing at Universal Studios. It was the first time I could show my parents part of my world as a motion picture director. It was also the first time that I pushed my mother in a wheelchair. Her walking had become limited as the result of a long illness. I felt my heart cringe each time I helped my mother transfer from the wheelchair to a chair on an attraction. Her once strong arms trembled, and her face tensed when she stood on her weakened legs. It was a strange contrast to be with my family in a park built for pleasure, and to be so conscious of my mother's pain.

Actors strolled by portraying characters like Laurel and Hardy, Mae West and The Director, who wore riding pants and boots and held a megaphone. The Director took one look at my mother in the wheelchair and said, "No more stunts for you!"

My mother burst into laugher, and my father and I joined her. It was delightful to see my mother's response. What was real here? My mother's pain and infirmity were real, but in just a moment our perceptions changed, and we enjoyed laughter and connection. Our revised perceptions helped us notice more than pain and infirmity in that particular moment.

My point is this: *It took just five words to change how we felt.* When you write down what you want, remember that just a few words can be powerful. And it's part of connecting with your True Self.

You are connecting with your True Self when you emphasize the good, the blessed and the abundance in the moment. Using a few powerful words gives you a pivot point for your thoughts and feelings.

It's the process of *Align with Your Design*.

Consider that whatever you write down immediately may be just the tip of the iceberg. For example, I might say I want to finish writing a children's book. But there's something deeper to it than that—which leads us to the second question ...

Momentum Action Plan (MAP)
Question 2: No. Come on, what do you really want?
Often, beneath our initial thoughts about what we want, there is something even more crucial that we want even more.

For me, what's below the idea of creating a children's book is that I really want to make a contribution to brightening the lives of millions of people—something like the joy inspired by Walt Disney.

And what's even deeper is this: I really want to feel I have accomplished a great purpose and that I've lived a meaningful life.

My clients have said:
- I want a new job. But what I really want is an end to the stress and meaninglessness of my current job.
- I want a closer relationship. But what I really want is to feel safe to reveal my deep feelings to my romantic partner.

You'll notice that we're talking about feelings. And that leads us to the third question ...

Momentum Action Plan (MAP)
Question 3: Better yet, what do you want to feel?

It's important to focus on what you want to feel. Remember the first four questions help you access your True Self. This third question gives us a special insight. What you want to feel is like an indicator light on a plane's control panel. This light reveals what your natural brilliance is.

In a previous section, I shared a quote from bestselling author Robert Allen: "When you're doing what you love to do, the money comes naturally. Maybe not at first, but eventually ... if you stick with it. Do you think Bob Hope started out with a goal, 'I want to become a millionaire by making people laugh, then I'll retire to do what I want'? I doubt it. He just did what he did best. And the money came."

We can imagine a moment or series of moments in which Bob Hope first made people laugh. He probably had the experience of "Oooh. I made them laugh. This feels good!"

Many of my clients have said, "I don't know what I want to do next with my life." The challenge then is to have them remember when they had an experience of "Oooh, this feels good!" We also need to remember moments of "Oooh, I'm good at this!"

Similarly, it may be time for my client to start trying new things to find out what brings the "Oooh!" feelings. How do you know if you will enjoy writing a song? You try it out.

How do you know if you will enjoy a cooking course? You attend a first class. By the way, I know a vivacious woman who has consistently tried new things and experienced success in different phases of her life. Let's look at her journey:

1. She began as a hair stylist.
2. She then owned her own salon. (15 years)
3. She sold the business and traveled the world.
4. She took an interest in graphic arts.
5. She earned a degree in graphic arts and worked as an administrative assistant in a church, using her graphic arts skills. (5 years)
6. Recently, she completed a program with the California Culinary Academy and has begun a career in the culinary arts.
7. In a few weeks, her first children's book will be completed.

It's important to know what you like; what feels good to you; what is fun for you. What feels great is often aligned with your natural brilliance. The idea is to align with your design. This means that you align with your gifts. Higher Power has given you natural brilliance and talents. It is up to you to experiment, to see how you feel, and then refine new skills.

Write down what you want to feel. Here's how this

process goes:

Sarah (a client): How do I know what I want to feel?
Tom: Good question. I'll help with a few questions. What do you want?
Sarah: I want to publish a children's story.
Tom: That's great! And what do you really want?
Sarah: I want to make money using my talents.
Tom: And if you can make money by using your talents, how would you feel?
Sarah: I'd feel … I'd feel safe. I'd feel like I could always take care of myself.
Tom: Great. Write that down. You want to feel safe.

Connect with desired feelings with "See, Hear, Touch"

Often, when we hear a question, our mind gives us the answer in flashing images, or sounds or a feeling. At one point, I listened to Serena, one of my college students with a major in Motion Pictures and Television Production. She described what motivates her with making feature films: "I see the audience clapping; I hear the audience's laughter; and I feel a warm hug (touch) from my brother as he celebrates the accomplishment with me."

So write down what you want to feel and note your impressions of See, Hear and Touch.

Write quickly. Don't hesitate. It's just you and the paper. Remember your initial impressions are usually on target.

By the way, you can keep your answers confidential. *Often, when a dream is new and fragile, it helps to avoid revealing it.* Some people, even family members, can torpedo a dream.

When Walt Disney wanted to create Disneyland, no one understood it. There had never before been a clean, delightful theme park. Walt's wife and his brother Roy were both against the idea. The Board of Directors was against it.

Walt had to cash in his life insurance to fund the initial research and design of Disneyland.

My point is that Walt Disney had an unusual faith in his own judgment, and many of us have not yet developed such a valuable faith. It may be best to keep quiet about our new dream until we have some tangible results in the right direction. For example, a friend of mine who is an associate editor of a magazine has recently completed a course in filmmaking. Two of the four films he made are quite effective. That's an important step forward.

The Momentum Action Plan that you're creating is for your eyes only (until you decide who is a real supporter of your dream). Now, let's continue ...

Momentum Action Plan (MAP)
Question 4: How to experience goals on a small scale?
At a particular speech, I held up a prop—a heart-shaped box. What's inside your heart? What do you want to feel?

One of my clients told me she wants to be an Oscar-winning actress. I asked her, "Where is the joy for you in acting?"

"It's being in the moment. Feeling the presence of the audience. Feeling the thrill of being alive and expressing my energy when I'm on stage. I had that experience in a high school production," she replied.

Write down this vital question: *Where is the joy?*

Answering this question helps you break free from previous patterns of thinking.

The idea of Free Yourself for Success is to think in a different way. The goal is to develop an entirely different pattern of thinking.

What you want to find is the element that creates the joy. When you know what creates joy for you, you can start experiencing that joy this week—on a small scale.

This week my client can sign up for an acting class. This week my client can borrow a video camcorder and practice a monologue in front of it.

It's important to get to the heart of the matter.

This reminds me of a time, some years ago, when I was directing a feature film. My cast and crew were on the set, which was an airport runway. This was before the September 11th tragedies, which is why my crew could be on a tarmac without any complications.

The heart of the matter for me when I'm directing is to keep everyone safe—and make a good movie. A stuntman was preparing to jump from an airplane before it left the runway. Everyone was unaware that the wing was headed straight for the cameraman's head. The plane's engines would drown out any possible warning. The cameraman was standing too tall. I had a split second to make a decision because no one else could help. A director is like a ship's captain, responsible for everyone's safety. I made my decision. I ran to the cameraman, grabbed him by the jacket and pulled him down. The wing sliced the air where our heads had been! What I learned that day was to keep a constant vigil and then act on what my intuition tells me. And I learned to keep focusing on the Heart of the Matter.

The first four questions of the Momentum Action Plan help you to access your True Self. To see how these elements fit together, let's look at this example:

Momentum Action Plan (MAP)—Partial Example
What do you want?
To complete writing my children's book.
No. Come on, what do you really want?
To uplift the lives of millions of people in ways similar to

what Walt Disney did.

Better yet, what do you want to feel?
To feel really alive. To feel the exuberance, a warm, full feeling in my chest (touch) when audience members laugh (hear) while watching an animated feature film I directed. To see big smiles as audience members rise from their seats at the end of the film.

How can you experience the heart (core elements/the heart of the matter) on a small scale?
The heart of the matter is to enjoy the excitement of collaboration—when people come together and make a "whole" that is better than the sum of its parts. I can enjoy the process of working with the artist, and guiding her to illustrate my story. I can enjoy the happy surprises when she returns with sketches that improve upon my initial ideas!

Now is your opportunity to pull all this together (and write your answers in your personal journal):

Momentum Action Plan (MAP)—so far
- What do you want?
- No. Come on, what do you really want?
- Better yet, what do you want to feel and note your impressions of See, Hear and Touch.
- How can you experience the heart (core elements/the heart of the matter) on a small scale?

A Special Note about What You Want
When you consider what you want, take a moment to put aside your thoughts and feelings that hold you back—like putting them into a drawer. Imagine that the Genie from Aladdin is here. You can have anything you want if you just write the details into your Momentum Action Plan.

My point is that once you voice what you want to feel and write it out where you can see it, you have made a major leap forward toward getting what you want.

Unfortunately, many of us will need to counteract our impulses to guard against disappointment and to avoid wanting too much. Please know that life brings disappointment no matter what. Playing small does not safeguard us from experiencing disappointment. But playing small does prevent us from enjoying surges of excitement and feelings of fulfillment that come with pursuing our dreams.

On the other hand, things flow better when you allow yourself to imagine big possibilities, and the universe provides you with some terrific, surprise opportunities. For example, years ago, as I walked down the corridors of the university I graduated from, I had a sudden feeling of I want to teach. Later, the father of one of the actors in a feature film I was directing alerted me to film related group and website. Through that website, I learned of a possible teaching position at a particular college. At the time of this writing I have been teaching graduate students and college students for a over 12 years.

The point of this story is to get in touch with what you want. When you do, you open the door to joyful possibilities.

Now, we are ready for the next question ...

Momentum Action Plan (MAP)
Question 5: How can you graduate up levels?
First, let's look at an example of my client who wants to be an actor. As a novice actor, she can:
- Take an acting class.
- Participate in Community Theater.

- Get a headshot (photo) made.
- Audition for local commercials.
- Make her own digital film that she can edit using her home computer. Or she can utilize the filmmaking talents of students at a local college.

Someone starting a business can plan out the steps needed to achieve a goal—that is, climb up a step and graduate to the next level. Let's say this person wants to become a professional speaker who sells products on the Internet.

She can:

- *Level One:* Give a free talk to a local association. Record the talk with a video camera and attach a microphone to her collar for the audio component.
- *Level Two:* Take the audio recording from the speech and download it onto a home computer. Make three copies of the speech by recording it onto CDs.
- *Level Two (part 2):* Take the three CDs to the next speech she gives to see if they sell.
- *Level Three:* Make more copies if the initial three CDs sell.
- *Level Four:* Consider writing a book based on the topic of the CDs she has been selling.
- *Level Five:* Write a book proposal to submit to an agent (who will submit it to a publisher).
- *Level Five (alterative):* Self-publish the book.

A person who self-publishes his or her first book is in good company: Deepak Chopra, Edgar Allen Poe, Sigmund Freud and many others have done just that. In fact, author Christopher Paolini, when he was 19-years-old (and with his parents' help), self-published the book *Eragon*. This book was made into a major motion picture.

The idea is to rise upward step by step. The question is *How can you graduate up levels?* If you don't know what the levels are, you can get a coach or listen to educational audio programs. Also, review your answers to Questions 1 through 4 to help you understand what you truly want, and your feelings about those desires. Then create a concise plan that will help you reach your next levels.

In order to make progress you need to stretch your comfort zone a little. But the important thing is to ease into doing new activities, which is covered in our next section ...

Momentum Action Plan (MAP)
Question 6: How can you gain an Immediate Victory?
The process for picking something that will be your Immediate Victory begins with preparation. Begin by writing down three easy things that will lead you in the direction of what you want. Make sure they're easy.

My clients have written:
- Do a Google search on the topic I'm interested in.
- Go to the bookstore and browse the books related to what I'm interested in.
- Get the book and read it for 15 minutes.

The Immediate Victory is a two-fold strategy: Focus on your successful action and then reward yourself for your accomplishment.

When you begin with easy victories and rewards, you feel encouraged to progress toward your goal.

During one interview, the host of a show said her reward was chocolate.

"I suggest that you have a menu."

"Of chocolate?" she replied, with humor.

I'm suggesting various rewards—and definitely some that don't involve calories.

In addition to writing down three easy tasks, write the rewards you want—so you have something to anticipate.

Rewards my clients have written include:
- A hot bath
- A phone call with my best friend
- To read my favorite fiction book
- To listen to an MP3 of my favorite singer

A reward is a wonderful way to encourage you to take more and more steps toward your goal. Starting with something easy prevents you from procrastinating. Researchers note that procrastination comes from fear and the anticipation of pain. Taking easy steps first helps eliminate both fear and concerns about pain.

Ease Into Momentum by starting with something easy. Reward yourself for your success. When you do your inner child says: "YES! This is great. I'll give you the energy to do more of this."

Your inner child is the part of you that feels small and vulnerable and wants to play. I emphasize that a strategy of Emotional Leverage is to make space to take care of your inner child. Find ways to be good to yourself and to include fun as part of your day.

Momentum helps you keep going. *You free yourself for success when you Ease Into Momentum.*

I call this process *The Easy Part Start.* If you want to write a book, you can start with an easy task: writing the chapter titles. That's what I do. Then I make a list of my anecdotes and a specific detail of research for each chapter.

The idea is to take action. Stop talking, and start doing.

Mother Teresa said, "There should be less talk; a preaching point is not a meeting point. What do you do then? Take a broom and clean someone's house. That says enough."

We are inspired to take a small step forward—The Easy Part Start. This reminds me of the old phrase: To know and not to do, is not to know. Let's take action ... and move on to the next question.

Momentum Action Plan (MAP)
Question 7: How can you announce what you offer?
Focusing on this question "How can you tell the world what you offer?" is a crucial step that many people leave out. There are those who would rather keep their heads down and just do their work. A number of artists and engineering-type people would prefer a world in which they just do a good job—and hope magically to get rewarded. But it doesn't work that way. People need to see you doing quality work.

In order to make your dreams come true you need to tell the world what you offer. And, the essence of telling the world is to clearly and concisely express what you're best known for. This is your personal brand.

The center of personal branding is this question, *"What am I best known for?*

When I think of *what am I best known for?* I think of this story Sam told in a job interview:

"I was hired to be a unit production manager for a feature film. The screenplay called for a bus. But the budget was strained. We needed a public place so that the romantic leads could meet by happenstance. A bus would require rental fees, hiring an off-duty police officer, hiring a bunch of extras, feeding everyone, and getting costly permits. I suggested the solution of having the two people meet in an elevator. Then I suggested that we could build an inexpensive elevator set in a living room using two by fours. The face of the producer lit up with relief. She told me,

"Sam, I can always count on you to solve a problem with creativity and to guard the budget. Good work."

So what do you think Sam is best known for? The answer is in the producer's comment. In essence, Sam solves problems with creativity and he guards the budget.

Sharing a story illustrates a desired characteristic, and this is a vital part of your personal brand.

Here are the elements of your personal brand:
- The answer to "what am I best known for?"
- A story that moves emotions
- A label
- A soundbite

Here's how Sam's might fill in his personal brand elements:

What am I best known for?

Solving problems with creativity and guarding the budget.

A story that moves emotions

Sam solves the problem for completing the feature film.

A label

Sam is a creative solution finder.

A soundbite

"Sam, I can always count on you to solve a problem with creativity and to guard the budget."

Find ways to effectively show what you offer. That's what Elijah Wood did when he wanted to play Frodo in the feature film trilogy *The Lord Of The Rings*. He had a friend videotape him wearing Hobbit clothes and doing an English accent. Elijah sent the videotape to the director Peter Jackson. That's how Elijah Wood came to star in the world-famous epic. By the way, *The Lord of the Rings III: The Return of the King* is the first fantasy movie in history to win Best Picture at the Academy Awards!

Remember that other people may influence the things you want:
- There's a job you want.
- There's funding you want.
- There's a movie role you want.

You need to effectively tell people what you offer.

That's the magic of an effective personal brand. Here are examples:
- My personal brand is Tom Marcoux, America's Communication Coach.
- Anthony Robbins calls himself America's Results Coach.
- Mark Victor Hansen uses the phrase America's Ambassador of Possibility.

An effective personal brand works in job interviews.

In a job interview, one of my clients used the phrase: "At XY Company, I was the go-to person for computers."

A personal brand makes you memorable. In a job interview a person could say: "I was called the Captain of Cost-cutting."

The idea is to give the interviewer the words she will repeat to her colleagues.

The interviewer will say, "Yes, Janet Smith is impressive. You know, she was known as the Captain of Cost-cutting at XY Company."

A personal brand involves a powerful story that moves emotions. For a job interview, plan to tell a story about how you saved the day using your skills or talents.

A personal brand quickly helps people get to know and trust you. It makes you stand out from other people.

Your personal brand improves your website.

On a number of occasions, I help my clients create a powerful personal brand that they present on their websites.

[For example, I helped one client start from zero and then have visitors (from 119 countries) to her blog.] I teach them to design their websites to provide visitors with a quick overview of who they are and what their services provide.

Websites need to answer the following questions that a web visitor has:

- *Question 1:* Who are you?
- *Question 2:* How can you help me?
- *Question 3:* How can you show you me that you're an expert?
- *Question 4:* How can you show me that you're trustworthy?
- *Question 5:* Why must I take action now? (It's best when you design a hyperlink that entices the web visitor to click immediately.)

Researchers have noted that people decide to leave a website within four seconds after arriving on a webpage—if their interest isn't grabbed immediately. Webmasters need to seize the attention of the web visitor. The above questions help them improve the design of their website—and attract visitors who will stay longer than four seconds. In the Internet world, establishing a personal brand is how to gain the visitor's trust and the person's business. In this way, prosperity can be expanded.

Here's another example of a personal brand: Tom Marcoux, The Personal Branding Instructor, as identified by *The San Francisco Examiner*. This example, which gives much more information about me, is almost similar to an endorsement.

Your personal brand needs to be true.

You need to be able to back up your personal brand with expertise. For example, my website has the domain name TomSuperCoach.com. When I started using that domain name I knew my friends and colleagues in the speaking industry would tease me about it. And they did send emails teasingly addressed to "Hey SuperCoach." Or, "Hello SuperTom."

There is a solution to the teasing: Live up to your personal brand. My domain name, TomSuperCoach.com, has proven to work because:
- I study everyday.
- I put in significant effort to provide helpful, effective coaching to my clients.
- I have a track record of guiding clients, audiences and readers to great results for over two decades.

Another point is the domain name of TomSuperCoach.com solves an important problem when I appear on television and radio. One TV host asked, "How does our audience get in contact with you?" When I replied "TomMarcoux.com," the host asked, "How do you spell Marcoux?" This is why my team came up with TomSuperCoach.com.

Problem solved, and a personal brand was created.

[Recently, I invite people to visit my blog at BeHeardandBeTrusted.com.]

Your personal brand is the method to effectively tell the world what you offer.

Momentum Action Plan (MAP)

Question 8: Say: "I want <goal> & my obstacle is <impediment>"

In my workshops, I hear audience members say:
- I want to start a business, but my obstacle is no money.
- I want to act and win an Oscar award, but my obstacle is I don't know anyone in the movie

industry.

In some of my speeches I show a graphic with a STOP sign. I change it into a START sign with just three letters: A-R-T. The art of making a breakthrough is to connect with people, ask questions, and get new ideas.

Now it's your turn. Fill in the blanks and write this down: I want <goal or desire> and my obstacle [to getting what I want] is <impediment>.

The idea is to talk to people about your goal—after you have taken some action steps in the right direction.

When you talk about your goal, you might hear someone say something like: "Oh, my cousin Stephen is an agent in Los Angeles."

One interviewer asked me, "How can I tell people what I want and the obstacle in front of it without sounding desperate?" I replied, "It's a matter of tone and timing. First, you listen to the other person. When you're listening, you're making rapport. Then, when the person asks 'What do you do?' you can reply with something like, 'At the moment, I'm a teacher. But what I'm really focusing on is moving my writing career forward. My obstacle is that I'm looking for a literary agent.'"

Here is an example of how connecting with one person can blossom into a big opportunity. When I began making films, many years ago, I didn't know anyone. To get started in the industry, I wrote a screenplay that I showed to a software engineer who passed it to another engineer. It then went to a real estate developer and finally to the California Motion Picture Commissioner. Three years later, when I directed my first feature film, the California Motion Picture Commissioner became my Associate Producer. He secured for me an airport and airplane—for free—for the film's production.

Remember to prepare so you can clearly express:

I want <goal or desire> and my obstacle [to getting what I want] is <impediment>.

Momentum Action Plan (MAP)

Question 9: Ask, "Give me suggestions, leads, wild ideas?"

To ask for suggestions, leads and wild ideas is an important part of getting a breakthrough. We need to get new ideas. We need the input of other people.

Participants in my workshops and seminars learn powerful ideas by sharing with each other.

Ask for input or feedback. *Ask someone. Ask Higher Power.*

The next process is something that I teach to my college students. I use a process I call *Choice Market Testing*™.

To get productive feedback, show someone two versions of something you're working on and ask these two questions in this sequence:

1. Which one do you prefer?
2. What about <the person's preference> grabs your attention?

Ask for help from Higher Power.

Jack Canfield came up with the title for his bestselling series *Chicken Soup for the Soul* by asking for God's help. He asked God to awaken him the next morning with bestselling titles. He woke up with the phrase "Chicken Soup for the Spirit" in his mind.

Remember to ask for help. A number of millionaires have said, "Wealth is a team sport."

Momentum Action Plan (MAP)

Question 10: Write due dates next to items on your list

We have now come to the final step in your Momentum Action Plan: Write a due date next to important items on your MAP. This is crucial. Remember this old phrase: A goal without a due date is just a wish.

This reminds me of a time when I was directing a feature film. When I'm directing a feature film, believe me, I'm under timeline constraints.

Here's the situation: I am on the set when a little 8-year-old actress, Kim, is expected to arrive at any moment. While I'm talking with my director of photography, a crew member calls out, "Kim's here."

I turn around, and my jaw hits the floor. There is Kim, with her timid little smile and a HUGE cast on her thumb. Broken thumbs were not in the script! So I tell everyone to Take 5, which means five minutes. I really want to say take five hours because I don't know what to do. So I sit down to rewrite the script. I immediately stand up and pace—trying to figure out what to do. After a while I come up with an idea.

I call the cast and crew to the set. The rewritten scene includes two brothers talking to each other. One brother is the father of Kim's character. The father had left the little girl in the care of his older brother. The older brother, disgusted with his brother's unchecked alcoholism, says, "Just in case you're interested, Kim broke her thumb!" Furious, the father pulls his fist back to slug his brother. Of course, the father is interested in his daughter's health! Just then Kim runs in, broken thumb and all, and says, "Daddy!"

I was relieved that my quick solution made the film better. When making a film, the director needs to adhere to a budget and schedule. In essence, the director has a due date every day in that a certain number of scenes must be filmed each day.

Having a due date makes you get creative. It helps you charge up with energy.

* * *

By filling in the details of the Momentum Action Plan (MAP), you have gone through the 9-Minute Miracle Breakthrough—although the training process probably took more than nine minutes. However, going forward, now that you know the process you can complete the Momentum Action

Plan for your week or month in nine minutes or less. You can make copies of the blank Momentum Action Plan form, which appears after the filled-in example (see the next few pages).

Momentum Action Plan (MAP)
(An example)

1. What do you want?

To complete my children's book which will lead to an animated feature film.

2. No. Come on, what do you really want?

To uplift the lives of millions of people in ways similar to what Walt Disney did.

3. Better yet, what do you want to feel?

See: The smiling faces of an audience watching the animated film I directed.

Hear: The applause of an audience during the closing credits of the film.

Touch: To shake hands with people who buy the children's book that accompanies the film.

I want to feel really alive. I want to feel the exuberance when audience members laugh while watching my animated feature film.

4. How can you experience the HEART (core elements/the heart of the matter) on a small scale?

The heart of the matter is to enjoy the excitement of collaboration—when people come together and make a "whole" that is better than the sum of the parts. I can enjoy the process of working with the artist, and guiding her to illustrate my story. I can enjoy the happy surprises when she returns with sketches that improve upon my initial ideas!

5. How can you graduate up levels?

Level One: Complete my children's book and make 25 copies.

Level Two: Obtain an agent and seek a publisher to publish a version of my book on a massive scale.

Level Three: Prepare for an animated feature—including storyboards and a budget.

Level Four: Seek to expand my circle of contacts and leads.

6. How can you do something easy and gain an Immediate Victory?

Go to Amazon.com and find a book on preparing an animated feature film. My reward can be an hour in a warm bath with soothing music.

7. How can you tell the world what you offer? (personal branding)

Come up with a soundbite to describe the children's book.

Come up with a memorable domain name.

8. Say: "I want <goal or desire> and my obstacle is <impediment>." (Tell someone.)

I want to produce and direct an animated feature film. My obstacle is to find funding sources.

9. Ask: "Please give me suggestions, leads, and wild ideas." (Ask someone. Ask Higher Power.)

Contact an association that supports uplifting media projects and ask them for the names of people who help film projects gain funding and support.

10. Write a due date next to an item on your list.

On March 19, 20__, I will contact the media association toward gaining contacts and leads.

* * * * * *

Momentum Action Plan (MAP)

To help you stay on track, complete this process on a weekly or monthly basis.

1. What do you want?

2. No. Come on, what do you really want?

3. Better yet, what do you want to feel?
See:
Hear:
Touch:

4. How can you experience the HEART (core elements/the heart of the matter) on a small scale?

5. How can you graduate up levels?

6. How can you do something easy and gain an Immediate Victory?

7. How can you tell the world what you offer? (personal branding)

8. Say: "I want <goal or desire> and my obstacle is <impediment>." (Tell someone.)

9. Ask: "Please give me suggestions, leads, and wild ideas." (Ask someone. Ask Higher Power.)

10. Write a due date next to an item on your list.

Copyright Tom Marcoux   BeHeardandBeTrusted.com

Prosperity is Founded on Relationships
Great Relationships Expand Financial Abundance

In a previous section, you learned the tools you need to wake up your spirit to prosperity. Then, we covered how to make plans to take powerful daily steps to create more prosperity in your life.

Now in this section, we focus on how to build and warm up your relationships through inspiring humor and laughter.

Enhancing relationships helps create the opportunities for wealth you desire. Humor is an important component. "Laughter is the closest distance between two people," said comedian Victor Borge.

The important thing to realize is this: *Real financial abundance is built on great relationships.* We often hear about the "big break," and many times that opportunity comes from a good relationship established years earlier. When you are committed to expanding prosperity, you are committed to improving your relationship-building skills. Here's an example:

On the set of a major motion picture, the Assistant Director was sweating bullets. Any delay meant $100,000 was being lost in wages, equipment rental and crew salaries. The Assistant Director turned to his crew members and, in a light tone, said, "Come on guys, let's pick it up a bit. You've got me looking at the Want Ads." The crew members moved faster, and the filming day was saved. Just the right tone and humorous words did the trick.

Learning to add humor helps you:
1. *Lead a team.* To create more abundance, we often find that we must become a leader of a team. "A sense of humor is part of the art of leadership, of getting along with people, of getting things done,"

said President Dwight D. Eisenhower.
2. *Inspire people.* Leaders need to inspire people. Great leaders use humor to build a community. "Laughter is the sun that drives winter from the human face," wrote statesman and novelist Victor Hugo.
3. *Improve your daily life.* "Humor is the great thing, the saving thing. The minute it crops up, all our irritations and resentments slip away and a sunny spirit takes their place," wrote Mark Twain.
4. *Enjoy giving and receiving love.* "We cannot really love anybody with whom we never laugh," noted writer Agnes Repplier.
5. *Diffuse anger.* "You cannot be mad at somebody who makes you laugh—it's as simple as that," said Jay Leno.
6. *Become resilient.* "Life is tough, and if you have the ability to laugh at it you have the ability to enjoy it," said Salma Hayek. Also, Albert Camus wrote, "In the depth of winter I finally learned that there was in me an invincible summer."
7. *Create a spiritual connection with people.* "Among those whom I like or admire, I can find no common denominator, but among those whom I love, I can: all of them make me laugh," emphasized poet W. H. Auden.

We can communicate well and create warmth in our relationships when we use humor to support our efforts. Often we hear, "She was a great speaker." Why? "Because she was funny, and she told great stories."

Here are methods to help you use humor. Humor is not merely telling jokes. Often, humor arises when emphasizing certain details in a story. Human beings are built to appreciate stories. An old phrase holds: "God created people because God wanted to hear stories." This chapter is based on my presentation, *Get Connected through Humor*.

Appropriate humor can warm up and deepen a relationship. We use the H.U.M.O.R. process:

H – Honor the personality style
U – Understand that no humor bit works for everyone
M – Mirror the person's humor preference
O – Open the door
R – Respect the person and environment

H—Honor the personality style

Our goal is to create rapport with other people. Before you use certain humor-creating methods, note the personality style of the person you are addressing. Here is an example of a behavior to avoid:

One time at an office supply store, the clerk made a client Stephen wait for a while, and then short-changed him. The manager was nearby and said, "Oh, that's how we get the money to order lunch." His attempt at humor completely broke a possible rapport with Stephen. Neither the clerk nor manager said, "I'm sorry for causing you inconvenience." That would have been appreciated because Stephen was under a deadline and lots of pressure. It would have been better if the manager had been respectful during their first encounter. Although his attempt at humor might have been well-intended, the manager's method of handling the situation was not appreciated. It would have been better to begin with an apology.

U—Understand that no humor bit works for everyone

No item of humor works on all people. It helps to have

ways to bounce back when the humor does not work. For example, once when speaking to over 300 people, I made a comment: "I wonder how Captain Kirk would handle this. Mr. Spock, raise the 'stress' shields." Some laughter. Still, I felt that my humor bit missed the mark. Then I said, "I guess that one was for the Trekkies." More laughter. That saved the moment. I generated two moments of laughter.*

[*Yes, I know that Star Trek fans prefer the term "Trekkers." For non-fans and to facilitate the humor bit, I had to use the other word.]

M — Mirror the person's humor preference

Roger Dawson, author of *The Secrets of Power Persuasion*, identifies five patterns of humor. And I will supply my example for each pattern:

- *Exaggeration:* A friend told me about a time when she was staying in a particular apartment building. She told someone: 'If these cockroaches get any bigger, I'll have to put them on a leash!'
- *Putdowns:* "And then Joe said, 'A martial artist? He couldn't kung-fu his way out of a paper bag!' " (I personally avoid putdown humor because it can cause trouble and hurt feelings.)
- *Puns:* I stand at work. The agony of the feet. (defeat)
- *Silliness:* In *The Pink Panther*, Peter Sellers does pratfalls.
- *Surprise:* Henny Youngman said, "Take my wife — please!"

Listen to the other person's preferences in humor. I have a friend who is a software engineer, and he loves wordplay. He is the only person I share puns with.

O—Open the door

Listen carefully to how the other person responds to something with a humorous tint. To open the door to humor: In the beginning, try small, gentle humor items. Perhaps, you might share an innocent cartoon from a local newspaper. See if the person chuckles, smiles, or fails to respond.

R—Respect the person and environment

I advise against using profanity. To many people, the only sure-fire environment where profanity usually fits in is a standup comedy nightclub. When using profanity outside a nightclub, be sensitive about the environment and the personalities that are present.

30 Secrets for Creating Humor

Secret 1: Prepare the Stage

In my college classes, I say a few things to help the students realize that appropriate humor will be part of my presentations. I mention that "humor will walk into the class at times, and go running out."

Secret 2: Notice that timing is acquired through practice

The secret to creating humor is to practice on safe audiences. Practice your humor on your loved ones and friends. Choose someone with whom you have a high comfort level. It is helpful to practice because successful expressions of humor require smoothness and comfort on your part.

Secret 3: Gain timing through subconscious modeling

We learned to talk through subconscious modeling when we heard our parents talk. Through them we modeled our behaviors.

Now the question is this: How do you get comedic timing

working for you subconsciously? Learn from stand-up comedians and by watching romantic comedy movies. When you're watching and enjoying these programs, you are subconsciously modeling the behavior of the comedians.

Secret 4: Play with words

When I visited the Comedy Warehouse in Walt Disney World, I witnessed comedians making up improvised humor. A comedian interviewed an audience member who met her fiancée through the Internet. The comedy troupe sang songs with these phrases:

- In Amsterdam—we'll go Dutch.
- She caught him in her net (Internet)
- You got a male (you got mail)

Secret 5: Use a good setup

At the Comedy Warehouse, the comedy troupe sang improvised songs. We, the audience, were told that the performance was improvised. However, as a comedy writer, I could see the pre-set structures. The performers knew certain music passages. The piano player had to know the pre-set song patterns. Also, the performers were using certain preset rhythms that I'm sure they practiced and rehearsed. Still, the audience laughed more and more because it was set up to believe that the performers were performing without a net.

Secret 6: Base humor on a song pattern

Some years ago, a friend and I waited and waited for a table at a restaurant. We were starving. I remembered the song by the rock band, Queen: "We will, we will rock you." Then, I sang to my friend, "We will, we will grovel!" I mimed begging for food.

Secret 7: Create a running joke based on the situation

In the situation when my friend and I were starving and waiting at the particular restaurant, I created three spontaneous bits of humor. The running joke was being hungry. The humor came from my voicing some exaggerated reactions to the hunger.

Secret 8: Base humor on icons, like *Star Wars*

While starving and waiting at the restaurant, I reminded my friend of a situation in *Star Wars: Episode IV: A New Hope* (the first one in 1977). Obi-wan Kenobi, the Jedi Knight, had used the Force to change people's minds. He said, "These aren't the 'droids you're looking for." Succumbing to Obi-wan's power, the Stormtrooper replied, "Uh, these aren't the 'droids we're looking for."

Since my friend and I were still waiting to be served lunch, I made the connection that we wanted the waiter (like a hypnotized Stormtrooper) to bring us our food. I said (like I was Obi-wan Kenobi): "You want to bring Tom and Sarah the food right now." Then, I said, like I was the waiter, "Oh, we're bringing the food right now." And the food arrived within seconds!

Secret 9: Enjoy understatement

At Walt Disney World, I watched a film about the art of animation. One animator who was balding and round said, "I was given Phil (in Hercules) to animate. He's short. He's bald. He's kind of fat. It's a stretch for me." Laughter rose from the audience. It was a triumph of understatement.

Secret 10: Tie-in experiences shared by the audience

At the Comedy Warehouse at Walt Disney World, a woman hesitated giving a book to a comedian. The comedian said, "You've got to give it back. There's nothing free at Disney." The crowd roared with laughter.

Secret 11: Choose a good target (perhaps yourself)

Denis Waitley, the best-selling author of *The Psychology of Winning*, uses himself as the target of humor. He speaks about the missteps he took when young and caught up in his

Ego. He talks about when he was a fighter pilot. He says, "I mowed the lawn in my flight suit—so the neighbors knew who they were living next to."

Secret 12: Remember to use context well

"There's nothing free at Disney" works so well because the audience spent (and I do mean spent) a whole day at Walt Disney World. This reminds me of a comment bouncing around the Internet: "Disney World is a people trap invented by a mouse." (As a sidenote: I really enjoy myself at Disney theme parks, so my comments are only intended as gentle humor.)

Secret 13: The Power-3 (context, structure, imposition)

The successful use of humor is about using effective patterns. Let's continue with the example "There's nothing free at Disney." *Context:* People spend money all day at Disney theme parks. *Structure:* The last word makes the joke funny. *Imposition:* The audience has feelings about being imposed upon by the pricing of Disney related items.

Secret 14: Twist a familiar phrase

Change a word and you make something funny. "Eat, drink and be merry, for tomorrow we economize." The original phrase is "Eat, drink and be merry, for tomorrow we die."

Secret 15: Set up the last word to have punch

Notice the last word in this example: "Take my wife—please!"

Secret 16: Go on a riff

A riff is a musical solo or a spontaneous improvisation. Here is an example: I was walking through Universal Studios, Florida, when I heard a rock and roll version of a classic Christmas song, "Oh, Holy Night." As my friend Sarah and I were listening to the song's phrase *Fall on your knees*, I said:

"That phrase Fall on your knees is one of the most powerful phrases in music—but not today.

"The melody is here; and the singer's somewhere over there.

"This is Sam's mother's favorite song. If she heard this version—she'd puke."

Let's notice that I went up the scale of intensity. I finished with an extreme word—puke.

Secret 17: Use the Magic of Three

In the above example we see the humor is structured in a pattern of three. The first statement sets up the situation. The second statement continues it. And the third statement twists the situation into a surprising direction.

Secret 18: Use the magic of the reoccurring joke

I once made a good rapport with a participant at a seminar. Because Joe demonstrated a good sense of humor, I made him the focus of some comments. He asked about the 15 judgments, a person makes about another person—which I call the four second barrier. I replied, "Someone meets you and thinks: nice suit, nice tie, needs Rogaine." Through the rest of the evening the comment about Joe's bald head became a reoccurring joke. Later I said, "What are the five forms of humor?" Joe replied, "Vicious"—and got a big laugh. I bowed Joe's way and said, "Forgive me."

Secret 19: Carefully use cynical humor

In the waiting area of the thrill ride Terminator 2: 3D at Universal Studios, Florida, TV monitors show mock commercials for the fictional company Cyberdyne (which, with no social conscience, created dangerous technology that destroys Terminator's world). The Cyberdyne commercial had a slogan: "We care so you don't have to."

Secret 20: Integrate current topics

One year, I witnessed the gruesome make-up show at

Universal Studios. A goofy special-effects teacher discussed the then just-released remake of the movie *The Mummy*. He said, "The prince is sealed in a tomb of flesh-eating Pokemon." The audience laughed with glee.

Secret 21: Make fun of a safe target

While standing in line for the thrill ride Terminator 2: 3D at Universal Studios, my friend and I (and the crowd) became tired of waiting. An actress came out and played the role of the public relations person for Cyberdyne, the unfeeling corporation that created the humanity-crushing technology. The actress played the part well. Her character spoke in phony, ingratiating tones—and had a grating habit of saying, "Superrr." At one point she said, "No applause necessary." I said to my friend, "And none will be heard."

Secret 22: Put in an Act Out moment

An Act Out moment is when the humorist acts out his routine instead of just standing and telling the story. A comedian who Acts Out another person will change his voice and posture to help the audience see the character. For example, if I was talking about a conceited CEO, I might perform (Act Out) his character. I would cross my arms, send my nose up into the air, and speak in a haughty tone. I would say: "I am a CEO. I know everything, I see everything, and I get indicted for everything."

Secret 23: Tie in the visual

At the Universal Studios gruesome make-up show, the goofy, special effects teacher pulled out a mannequin that looked like a shark had eaten half its body. He said, "This is Barbie. We have a special on Barbie today—half-off." The audience rocked with laughter.

When on vacation in the South of France, one of my friends heard another traveler commenting on vacationers' tendency to overeat. The traveler said, "If I eat any more I'll have to grease my legs to get my pants on."

Secret 24: Rehearse your choice of words before telling a story

Often a good story sounds better with concise words. Rehearse key phrases. Here is an example:

A man was getting tired of his wife always saying "Turn around, I think I left the iron on" when they were driving away, leaving for their annual trip. The next year, like clockwork, she waited until they were two miles away from home. She said, "Go back, I think I left the iron on." At a stoplight, the man pulled the iron from beneath his seat.

Notice how the story is told with few words.

Secret 25: Use similar sounds

One time on vacation, I turned to my loved one and said, "Ahh, what a sight to see: A flamingo doing the flamenco." She chuckled.

Secret 26: Use rhythm

Rhythm is a helpful component in humor. Here is an example expressed in the book, *The Healing Power of Humor*. Joan, a hospital nurse said, "I'm a body scratcher, patcher, wire attacher and bed pan snatcher."

Secret 27: Note goofy items from the newspaper

An essay contest in England entitled *Buy Britain* gave out prizes: radios made in Japan.

Secret 28: When speaking, use topic-oriented cartoons

When giving a presentation, it's easiest to warm up the room by placing cartoons on an overhead projector at the start of your talk. In this way, you don't have to worry about finding the right joke to set the tone of your presentation.

Secret 29: Use a label as you tell a story

I was coaching a client who wanted to make her story funnier. She mentioned a mean teacher at school who ate wasabe (the Japanese horseradish condiment). I suggested she label him Wasabe-breath.

Secret 30: Ad-lib in the moment

At a hospital, giving a presentation on *Say YES to Yourself: Successful Strategies for Conflict and Change in the Workplace*, I talked about working with a blunt, hard-charging director. In the moment, I improvised this comment: "Tell the bottom- line Director, 'The patients are still alive. It's a good day.'" The audience laughed.

Abundance is Built on Great Relationships

We warm up and deepen relationships with appropriate humor. Becoming skillful with expressing humor is worth every effort you make. For example, for years I have shown a particular film clip to my students of my college course Science Fiction and Fantasy. The film clip is a scene from the feature film *The Abyss*, directed by James Cameron. The lead character "Bud," portrayed by Ed Harris, is introduced while he leads his team.

He gently, and with humor says, "Hey Harry. Do me a favor, will ya? Square away this mud hose, get rid of some of these empty sacks. This place is starting to look like my apartment."

Bud uses humor to guide his team members to keep the work area safe.

My students consistently say that they like Bud. And this illustrates my point: appropriate humor warms up relationships.

With better relationships, you *wake up your spirit to prosperity*.

For example, this book was completed with editing work from some of my friends. One I have known and trusted for 19 years, and another for 24 years. And yes, we laugh together often.

Try experimenting with various forms of humor. Practice on safe audiences.

BOOK THREE: THE LAW OF ATTRACTION – ADDITIONAL TOPICS

For wealth creation and for manifesting loving relationships, the Law of Attraction forms a crucial component. In this section we'll cover these topics:

1) Get Unstuck! Use the Method: "Don't Replicate; Innovate"
2) Secrets You Can Use to Handle Fear and Really Succeed–and Enjoy Life!
3) Stay Strong and Get through Grief with Grace
4) Nonattachment and "Beware the Creeping Gray"

1) Get Unstuck! Use the Method: "Don't Replicate; Innovate"

Have you noticed that fear keeps us stuck? The Law of Attraction holds that if you spend too much time in fearful thoughts and feelings you will merely attract more fear!

At one point, I learned something *really important* about fear and getting unstuck.

To deal with fear, observe your first impressions, but do *not* stop there.

For example, one of my big fears is "wasted time." My time is full with work on my franchise *Jack AngelSword* and teaching graduate students and college students.

Now, imagine that you want to do something that can improve your career and that can help other people—But you do *not* feel you have the time.

That was my feeling in this particular situation: One of my focus areas is providing high-end coaching to a select clientele. The problem is (and here's where the fear of wasted time comes in): traditional sales techniques often involve a LOT of sales presentations that end in hearing the word "No." Unfortunately, such sales presentations that end in "no" feel like "wasted time" to me.

Further, attending networking events is often a go-to plan for someone selling a high-end service.

So this appears to be a conundrum. How can I be in two places at the same time? That is, how can I focus on my full schedule and still find new clients for my high-end coaching?

If I just focus on standard "sales techniques," I would just drop the whole idea of reaching new high-end coaching clients due to my lack of extra time.

Here's the solution:

Don't Replicate; Innovate.

After I observed my concern about "wasted time," I paused. Then I thought about DIFFERENT ways to introduce my high-end coaching to prospective clients.

Now, **my preferred way to gain a new coaching client includes this process:**

1. The prospective client sees my new 2 min. 40 second video. Instead of just a commercial; the video offers **valuable methods.** (Always make sure that the person gets value from interacting with you.)

2. The person calls my office. During the phone call, I pre-qualify the person by asking **three questions.**

3. I offer only five unique free coaching experiences per month—and such an experience is only available for qualified prospective clients.

All of the above conserves my time. The truth is: I take on few coaching clients. My service as a coach is in small supply.

Using a video saves a lot of time. For example, people can be watching the video while I'm asleep. (**During the video I provide a SOLUTION to a misconception about performing at your best during tough situations.** You can find this video on YouTube by typing "Tom Marcoux Reveals to Perform at Your Best".)

My point is: **You and I do NOT have to remain stuck in our fearful thoughts and impressions.**

We can do something new.

Yes, we'll need to step forth from our comfort zone.

We'll need to try new methods. Some of them will work and some will need to be refined. And likely, some experimental methods will need to be dropped.

I invite you to avoid dropping a new project just because your first impressions bring up fearful thoughts.

Remember: **Don't replicate; Innovate.**

2) Secrets You Can Use to Handle Fear and Really Succeed–and Enjoy Life!

Have you noticed that fear can stop you in your tracks? Fear can actually shutdown a positive pattern of thinking. The Law of Attraction reminds us to avoid letting ourselves stay stuck in fearful thoughts and fearful feelings. Otherwise, you'll attract more things in your life that inspire fear.

I'm really glad to share the following methods to help you release yourself from fear.

First, we need to be aware that fear can shutdown our ability to think of options—and that can kill success You can observe that successful outcomes depend on *prior* successful thoughts and actions. I've learned a lot about handling fear as a feature film director, actor, guest instructor to MBA students at Stanford University, and entrepreneur in many tough and fear-inspiring situations. When you do anything that has high stakes, it helps to set successful patterns in *yourself* so you can perform at your best. We'll use the W.I.N. process:

W – will the power into Your Second Thought

I – increase flexibility (power of rehearsal)

N – nurture adaptability

1. Will the power into Your Second Thought

The verb will relates to "expressing determination, insistence, persistence."

We see this clearly when someone says, "I *will* walk for 30 minutes at lunchtime today."

Certainly that's more powerful than a wishy-washy phrase like: "I *hope* to walk for 30 minutes."

Let's look at how we can use the power of "I will" when it comes to handling fear.

Anytime you're going to do something for the first time, it's natural for fearful thoughts to arise. Someone may turn down a chance to give a speech because of the thought: "I'll choke up. I'll feel humiliated." Many people stop with this first fearful thought.

On the other hand, I now invite you to develop **The Power of Your Second Thought.**

In fact, it would be great for you to say, "I *will* develop the power of my Second Thought."

We may not be able to stop a first fearful thought from arising, but *we have the choice* to condition ourselves so that the *next thought* turns us toward an empowering direction.

Condition yourself to make Your Second Thought powerful.

How to Condition Yourself:

1) First, you need access to lots of empowering ideas.

Read books, listen to audiobooks, attend workshops and see empowering videos. Learn from people who have accomplished what you want to do.

2) Write down and often review empowering ideas.

I take this another step further; I memorize empowering ideas. I memorize some phrases that I've written for my books including: "Keep score and achieve more." "Courage is easier when I'm prepared."

I also memorize other quotes written by others:

One can never consent to creep when one feels an impulse to soar. – Helen Keller

Here's an empowering phrase that I devised and an image to help my clients and college students become better public speakers: Picture a kind grandmother saying, "Feeling fear? Rehearse my dear."

I invite you to use this as your Powerful Second Thought. If you feel fear, remind yourself: "Feeling fear? Rehearse my dear."

2. Increase flexibility (power of rehearsal)

When you rehearse, you instill new patterns in your mind and in your body. When we first learn to do something, we feel awkward. After lots of rehearsal, we become good. We're even able to do some things well *unconsciously.*

I've studied acting, martial arts, public speaking, piano-playing, writing and more. All of this study and rehearsal has helped me perform at my best—even when I was scared.

For example, years ago, I arrived for a photo shoot for a top software company's website.

The photographer took one look at me and with a big frown said, "Oh. You were born in America." He had previously picked my headshot photo and had apparently wanted an Asian man born in an Asian country.

His reaction made me really afraid that I would be dismissed. I had spent funds on getting to the location and I did need to earn money that day.

Because of my training and rehearsal, my mind was flexible. I immediately said, "How about I put my hands like this. Like a Buddhist monk?"

I changed my posture from "brazen, shoulders thrown back, born-in-America guy" to humble, spiritual, calm guy.

"That will work," replied the photographer and he snapped a number of photos. He then paid me $400. That was the first time, I earned $400 in one hour.

For me that's the power of flexibility to help one in a scary situation.

3. Nurture adaptability

From years of rehearsing and giving speeches, I've developed my skills to answer spontaneous questions from the audience.

Effective action builds your confidence. You learn that you are flexible and that you adapt well.

Confidence is *not* about feeling comfortable.

It's about *knowing from experience* that you are flexible and that you adapt to various situations.

For example, I stood giving a speech to an audience at Sun Microsystems. One audience member asked, "What do you do when your boss does NOT listen to anything you say?"

For a moment, I was stumped. I was afraid.

But on the outside, *due to my rehearsals and developing my own techniques,* I said, "Julie, I can see that's important to you. I might need to pause for a moment. I want my comment to be useful for you."

By the time, I had finished saying this, my mind (working

at about 700 words a minute*) found the answer: I said, "Quote your boss back to him. Then express what you want to say. Someone like your boss only cares about his own opinions and his own words. Fine. Say back his words to him. Then you'll have his attention, and then add your own idea."

[*Researchers suggest that human brains tend to operate at about 700 words a minute.]

So how do we deal with fear? We develop our own adaptability.

Another way to remember how to deal with fear is what I call *"ALF – Adapt, Learn, Flex."*

To create the joy, success and fulfillment you want, *rehearse and develop your skills to handle fear*. And the bonus is: you simply enjoy more moments everyday!

3) Stay Strong and Get through Grief with Grace

Would you like to somehow stay strong even when you are confronted with grief? The Law of Attraction invites us to flow into each present moment. Grieving is a natural part of life. And still, it helps to *not* get stuck. I've learned that I can feel grief for some moments off and on during the day — and still have some joy.

It is helpful to develop a healthy pattern when dealing with grief.

Yes, it can be a struggle to keep doing your job well enough and still give yourself the space to feel your feelings. Now, here's a process to help you stay strong and also "grieve with grace." For my clients, I have identified actions that can help you navigate your way through the grieving process. Here is the process:

C – contain
O – open to a Soothing Activity
M – move
F – focus through "good pace music"
O – offer helpful times and places
R – replace distractions
T – talk out feelings
S – support yourself (learning and some laughter)

1. Contain

My client Jerrie said, "I can't cry now. Once I start crying, I don't think I'll be able to stop. I work with some 'macho guys' and I'll look weak if I cry in front of them."

I replied, "Let me share a couple of ideas and you might find one or more of them to be helpful." At that point, I mentioned the value of having a "container for your grief." By this I meant: pick some time during the week to actually grieve. If you try to avoid all grieving, it can twist you up inside. Further, it may bubble up exactly at the wrong moment, such as when you're in front of people at work. They could misinterpret your emotional outburst as an overreaction to something in the workplace (instead of your personal grieving).

Fortunately, my client Jerrie *set up a recurring Saturday therapy appointment* so she could cry out her feelings in a safe environment. After each therapy session, she took a walk to calm down. The physical activity also served as a transition before she continued with her day off.

2. Open to a Soothing Activity

By *Soothing Activity*, I mean an activity that gives you a break from your grief AND *fills your mind*. For example, I often work on a jigsaw puzzle while either listening to music or a stand-up comedian's routine. I find this to be a time to slow down and enjoy myself.

I mentioned "fill your mind." For some of us, meditation during grief is painful. Why? We slow down and our mind fills up with memories and painful thoughts. That's why I like to pick a Soothing Activity that engages my mind. For some, reading, singing or playing a musical instrument helps.

3. Move

Physical exercise can help you drain stress from your body. I often read and walk on a treadmill simultaneously. I find that reading takes my mind off the exercise and the time duration of the exercise routine.

4. Focus through "good pace music"

If you're concerned about focusing your mind for work, condition yourself to respond to "good pace music." By this I mean, some fast-paced music can speed up your efforts; for example, you can file paperwork at an efficient pace.

5. Offer helpful times and places

Using a timer can help you step into different "phases" during your day. If you're feeling sad, you might devote "the next 20 minutes to listening to sad songs." Then when the timer chimes, you can take a walk.

Sometimes grief robs us of energy. So you might use the timer to "focus for five minutes on paying bills." If there is a *set time with a limit*, we can often get ourselves to do an onerous task.

A place can serve as a trigger for certain feelings. Choose your triggers, that is, *choose a place with ca*re. If staying in the apartment you shared with a former partner brings you down, choose to step outside each day. Perhaps, take a walk at a nearby park or read a book at a local cafe. At some point, you might choose to move to another building or even another city.

If you need to get some work done, pick a particular chair and table to do your work. In essence, you condition yourself to get right to work when you're in a particular place.

My point is that you need to take extra care while you're grieving. You'll likely experience less energy so carefully arrange your schedule. Pick helpful times and places so you're able to function as you go through the necessary grieving journey.

6. Replace distractions

When you are grieving, you are likely in pain much of the day. So what do we do? We grab at any distraction available. Such a distraction robs us of time and can even put our job in jeopardy. Instead, consider working on a report by using your laptop (or mini-computer) with your Wi-Fi turned off. In this way, you'll have the chance to work on something without checking your email every couple of minutes. Be careful about distractions. It's reported that many people check their smartphones 150 times a day. Replace distractions and get the most important things done.

7. Talk out feelings

To whom can you turn and truly express your feelings? In the past, I've avoided burdening my friends with repeated heavy-emotional talks.

Instead, I've hired my own coaches and consultants for insight and times to talk about heavy issues.

If you're going through a truly tough time, consider

hiring a therapist or counselor.

The truth is: If you can talk out your feelings, you'll press on through the grieving process. (I use the words "talk out" because it's helpful to get the feelings out into the open, to unburden your heart and to be able to "see them."]

On the other hand, if you don't talk out your feelings, you are likely postponing your pain and anger. Leaving pain and anger to fester can cause a serious disruption. Don't let that happen. *Find healthy ways to talk out your feelings.*

8. Support yourself (learning and some laughter)

Currently, I'm experiencing the process of supporting my mother in the last chapter of her life. This process is all new to me so *it's time for me to learn how to work with this situation.*

If you're going through a big grieving time, you might find a lot of support from reading books or listening to an audiobook. Let's face it. When something is tough and new to you, it really helps to hear how others endured and triumphed. To support myself, I purchased a highly recommended book by a gerontology expert who supported her mother in the last chapter of life. As you can see, I took action to find a resource in someone who had already dealt with this same tough situation.

Now, I'm adding a detail that may, at first, seem unusual. Consider finding chances for you to experience a bit of humor. I'm actually systematic about this. Every day, I see something funny on video at YouTube or via my digital video recorder (like TIVO). Why? Laughter releases endorphins and lowers one's stress levels.

I've noted that people experience moments of laughter even at funerals. These moments provide valuable relief!

4) Nonattachment and "Beware the Creeping Gray"

To really invoke the Law of Attraction in your life, it helps to practice nonattachment. Nonattachment includes holding preferences in your life but not staying stuck in "making demands."

For example, I may prefer that my friend Tami says kind things to me on a particular day, but I do not demand it. Perhaps, on a particular day, Tami is distraught over the ending of a romantic relationship. In her despair, she is abrupt with several people.

I am nonattached. I calmly view the situation as, "Tami is in pain and she's doing the best she can."

If I were attached to insisting that Tami act "perfect," I might turn off the Law of Attraction. How? It would keep me in a rigid, upset state of mind.

Instead, I seek to flow with each moment.

I'll now share the process . . .

Uncomfortable in her hospital bed after neurosurgery, my mother started coughing. It felt like another insult to her injury . . . and a few hours later Robin Williams would gasp his last breath.

I'm mourning. My mother is in the last chapter of her life. This time is rough on her. Also today (8-11-14) Robin Williams ended his life. When an artist dies, I get sad about the ending of that artist's creativity. No more comedic lines to get us laughing. No more movie roles for the world to enjoy.

One thing that I have noticed is that each time I'm about to step into the hospital room where my mother lies so small and vulnerable, I feel dread. What's going to happen next? What am I going to see? Is she still going to be in restraints that stop her from pulling a feeding tube out of her nose?

So I start thinking in ways that create a low mood. I dread moments in advance. I dread calling my mother or talking with my father in anticipation of more bad news. This could be summarized as a fear of "what's next?"

However, I'm going to modify "What's next?" with something positive. I'll change it to *"What's next?—It might be good."*

This is my new *defiant stance.*

It's too easy to allow the dread of what bad things that *may* happen to color one's experience in the present moment. I call it *"The Creeping Gray."* (It bleeds *the life* out of us.)

Worry creates The Creeping Gray. Worry is NOT helpful.

A plan can be helpful. Action can be helpful. But anticipating pain before you step into the situation just ruins your present moment.

So I mention my defiant stance of "What's next?—It might be good." I've learned that we often *cannot* control the first thought that arises, but we can control what we do with it.

I'm interested in "The Power of the Second Thought."

In this situation, I turn around my first dread-filled thought of "what's next?" by *adding* **"It might be good."**

Things can become better and surprise you. For example, before my mother's surgery her hands and legs stopped working. She was bedridden. Now, after the neurosurgery her hands are stronger and she can lift her legs. So she might be on the road of recovering a lot of her ability to move. I hope so!

Some people are afraid to hope. They're afraid to have their hopes dashed.

Instead, I want to *avoid* living with no hope, just in the midst of "The Creeping Gray."

Now I invite you to observe yourself and your thoughts.

- Are you living a life of "gray"?
- Are you avoiding thoughts of hope because you are too afraid of having your hopes dashed?

Perhaps, you may want to adopt the phrase: ***"What's next?—It might be good."*** (Or it might be okay. Or it might be something that tests you and forces you to become deeper as a human being. It might make you more compassionate.)

You might find that you can your spirits up in this present moment if you adopt the defiant stance of "What's next?—It might be good."

Author Will Bowen emphasizes that life is meant to be challenging because "it keeps us engaged and growing."

I've learned that *I grow more by staying in the present moment.*

If I jump ahead to worries about the future, I use mental discipline to bring myself back to the present moment.

The present moment is the only thing we truly have.

Stay present. Stay flexible. Experience good moments.

BOOK FOUR:
THE LAW OF CREATION – ADDITIONAL TOPICS

For wealth creation and for manifesting loving relationships, the Law of Creation forms a crucial component. In this section we'll cover these topics:
1) Release the Brakes: Use the 30-30-30 Shield
2) Secrets So You Keep Going When You Feel "On Empty"

1) Release the Brakes: Use the 30-30-30 Shield

I've learned from working with 5,241 college students and graduate students that a number of people are slowed down by fear. Fear functions like a parking brake.

Do not keep it engaged. Instead, release the brake!

I've learned to use a method that I call *"The 30-30-30 Shield."*

Using this method began when I came across a particular quote:

When asked how she deals with a lot of pressure (as pro athlete, *Sports Illustrated* model, mother and wife of celebrity surfer Laird Hamilton), Gabrielle Reese said, "In life, you will always have 30 percent of the people who love you, 30 percent who hate you and 30 percent who couldn't care less."

We can use the above quote as part of what I call the "30-30-30 Shield." How?

The ideas of Gabrielle's quote release us from trying to be perfect and from trying to please everyone.

Many of us experience a huge drop in energy and motivation when under-fire by others' criticism.

Your first thoughts might be on the order of: "Oh, no! I can't do anything right. Nobody's going to like my book, my blog, my artwork, etc."

Instead, invoke your 30-30-30 Shield.

You can assess: "Is this person part of the 30 percent who will never understand the value of what I'm doing? Are they someone who will never care? If so, *I can dismiss them* from my mind."

With the above, you could even "shield" your self-esteem. When someone slams criticism at us, it can feel like a blow to our self-esteem.

But with the 30-30-30 Shield we can assess: "This person just doesn't care about what I care about." or "Evidently, I made artwork that does not appeal to this person. I'll serve my own audience."

We can devote more time to thinking about the 30% who do love us:

Being deeply loved by someone gives you strength, while loving someone deeply gives you courage. – Lao Tzu.

In summary, guide your own thoughts. Don't let them fall into a negative spiral. Instead, employ your 30-30-30 Shield and rejoice in being fully alive. Experiment with creativity, take appropriate risks and concentrate on those people who can relate to your style of creativity. In this way, you have the Law of Creation functioning at full throttle in your life.

2) Secrets So You Keep Going When You Feel "On Empty"

"I can't keep going," my friend Trudy said, her eyes tearing up. "I've lost all the enthusiasm I had for writing my children's book. My inspiration's dried up. What was I thinking, anyway? This is just another project that I've started and stopped," Trudy continued.

Like many of us, Trudy stumbles and quits on her own project.

How about you? What new thing have you tried? Losing weight? Taking some classes? Have you had setbacks and have you given up?

Over the years, *I had to become an expert* about persisting and finishing projects.

Persistence turns out to be an important topic for my clients and college students. I'm not going to give you mere theories. As an author of 25 published books, I'll now share *Methods That Work*—not just theories. We'll help you be ONE of the few people who get big things done.

We'll use the O.N.E. process:

O – open to accountability

N – nurture breaks

E – enjoy progress (rewards and more)

1. Open to accountability

At the beginning of a project, it's often exciting. We're filled up with joy about possibilities. The creativity flows easily. Team members are excited.

Then there's a time in the middle of the project when it becomes "just work."

This is okay. If you know that you will endure a bumpy patch in the road, *you'll prepare for it!*

Patience, persistence and perspiration make an unbeatable combination for success. - Napoleon Hill

I encourage my clients and students to develop *"an Empowering Accountability."* By this I mean, you have a friend celebrate with you each step forward especially when it's hard. This can be as simple as leaving an email (for your friend) before you start a 20 minute session of writing. Then after you finish that 20 minute session, you send an email confirming that you kept your word and finished the writing session.

Your friend responds with something like: "Well done! Good work. You're getting closer to done. Good for you!"

A little more persistence, a little more effort, and what seemed hopeless failure may turn to glorious success.
– Elbert Hubbard

Between goals and achievement are discipline and consistency.
– Denzel Washington

Set up your own schedule. Be accountable to yourself. Keep a Progress Log.

Get started. A paragraph each day. One drawing a day. A lot can be done with a little bit each day. One year of drawing a day yields 365 drawings for an entire year. In this way, you energize the Law of Creation in your life.

2. Nurture breaks

Turning from the white board to my college students, I said, "Take breaks or be broken." I then asked the illustration majors in the class, "Have you had an instructor suggest that you back away from your illustration and turn your head sideways or even turn the image upside down?"

Four students said, "No."

"No?!" I replied. "Then you're hearing one now."

I went on, "What do you get when you look at the image sideways?"

"A new perspective," two students replied.

Exactly. That is what a break can do for you! More than that, *a break can renew your energy* and even your feelings of hope.

Here Is Another Form of Taking a Break

Consider letting people know when you're on a roll and

have momentum. In appropriate circumstances, you might say, "I'm in the middle of big deadlines. Please feel comfortable to contact me on ____ [10 days later.]"

I call the above practice a way of *"getting a break* from other people crashing down on your schedule."

If you're working on a personal project, you'll likely be considered odd (or even "obsessive") by family and friends.

Author Stephen King, at 67 says, "I still write everyday." He's completed and published 55 novels. That takes focus, effort and time.

Energy and persistence conquer all things. – Benjamin Franklin

Benjamin's idea may or may not apply, but I ask you: "How many people get something big done without energy and persistence?" . . . I rest my case.

Taking breaks provides a renewal of energy.

How can you take regular breaks?

3. Enjoy progress (rewards and more)

At this moment, I'm 53 days into one book project and I'm 37 days into another book project. Yes, I'm logging details because *I give myself credit* for my persistence.

I invite YOU to give *yourself* credit: Use a *Progress Log*.

And even reward yourself when you hit small milestones. Don't wait for anyone to reward you. You create your own mini-celebrations. It can be as simple as getting a cup of coffee or meeting with a friend.

At the end of our lives we all ask, "Did I live? Did I love? Did I matter?" – Brendon Burchard

The truth is: You are the one person who will most affect the course of your life. *You're the one* to come up with methods that work. Try some methods, use them and get new ones if they stop working for you.

I have no trouble dropping methods when they don't

work, anymore. Why?

Because I think of life as a series of chapters.

Some methods work in your current daily routine. Then you move on to new techniques in the next chapter of life.

Never underestimate the power of the simple Progress Log to power up the Law of Creation in your life.

Glancing up I see my *5 Progress Logs* next to my computer monitor.

If you don't write 1,000 words a day, you're not serious about writing. – John Grisham

That works for John Grisham.

I suggest, if you're writing (or running), you can build up slowly.

It does not matter how slow you go as long as you do not stop. – Confucius

Doing a big project is a marathon.

Take strategic breaks.

Be sure to "refuel your creativity tank." [Yes, I do retreat to a Disney Park every so often.]

See films, read books, do a puzzle, take a walk among trees, or anything else that helps you relax and feel an intrinsic joy.

Keep going.

BOOK FIVE:
THE LAW OF BEING –
ADDITIONAL TOPICS

For wealth creation and for manifesting loving relationships, the Law of Being forms a crucial component. Sometimes, I view the Law of Being as "The Law of Renewal."

Additionally, the Law of Being includes ways for you to have a healthy, empowering mindset so you avoid losing personal energy. In this section we'll cover these topics:
1) How to Believe in Yourself When Others Don't
2) Improve Your Life and Relieve Yourself of Needless Suffering
3) Find Your OWN Path to Big Success and Lasting Happiness

1) How to Believe In Yourself When Others Don't!

Would you like to claim a gift that is uniquely yours? The gift is a nourishing belief when those around you fail to see your vision. We'll use the A.I.M. process:

A – acknowledge it's *your* destiny and not theirs
I – identify with your intuition
M – measure by your heart and NOT their approval

1. Acknowledge it's *your* destiny and not theirs

Here's a way you can *stay strong* even when you feel all alone and deeply disappointed that loved ones do *not* support you in *your* making your dream come true.

Perhaps, like many people, your loved ones are *afraid*. Maybe on a subconscious level they're afraid that you will get hurt as you step out of your comfort zone. Or even, *they feel uncomfortable* being around someone so focused and striving to fulfill his or her potential. Maybe they fear that you'll change and leave them behind when you do succeed on a significant scale. Sometimes we lose friends. Top author and speaker Larry Winget wrote: "Some friendships are like belts. We outgrow them."

Here's an important point to realize: *Other people cannot feel what you feel or intuitively know what you know.* Why? It is YOUR destiny—not their destiny. You're the one person who has all the clues and internal signs that your idea is a valuable one.

Perhaps, you've felt the gut-wrenching disappointment when a loved one does *not* support you in your pursuit of something that's close to your heart.

There is an answer to this. A neighbor of mine who races motorcycles competitively said, "In motorcycle racing, we're trained with the idea: *If in doubt, gas it out."* The idea is to "pour on the gas." My neighbor assures me that if there's an irregularity in the road, more gas will help the motorcyclist get over the small ridge.

How can we apply *if in doubt, gas it out?* First, look to yourself for confirmation and energy. Add things that empower you. Often, when I'm writing I'm listening to empowering music. I read empowering books and I see uplifting films.

The point here is: You must take action to keep up your own spirits.

2. Identify with your intuition

Above, I invited you to listen to yourself for confirmation.

Just because someone close to you cannot see or imagine your idea, it does NOT mean that they're right! It just means that they cannot feel the value of your idea.

Identify with your intuition and *not* their fears.

Many things that turn out well took time. For example, it took 8 years and many studios turning down the feature film *Splash* before it was produced, and Ron Howard directed the film. In fact, Disney turned it down the first time, and it was not until Disney *created a new division*, Touchstone Pictures, did *Splash* (starring Tom Hanks and Darryl Hannah) get made.

A truly famous example is how co-authors Mark Victor Hansen and Jack Canfield held to their intuition and endured 140 rejections before their book *Chicken Soup for the Soul* was published. The *Chicken Soup for the Soul* series has resulted in 250 additional titles and more than 500 million books sold.

Go by your intuition. Do not rely on others to "have all the answers." So-called experts can be wrong. You may be providing something that is new and different.

How can you recognize your "voice of intuition?"
Here's a quick description of two "voices."
- Voice of fear: contract, hide, do not experiment
- Voice of intuition: expand, build, take appropriate risks

Every day and really every moment, we have a choice. We can grow and expand and step toward our destiny. Or we can contract and hide and let doubters bring us down.

I invite you to *nurture yourself and step forward* into a steady pace to create something new and better in your life.

3. Measure by your heart and NOT their approval

In a way, I've been lucky that my father is stuck, for decades, in a disapproval mode. **I've learned to listen to my**

own heart and ignore his negativity. The truth is he has had no experience related to being an entrepreneur, graduate school instructor, author, and feature film director. Sure, he has opinions—*uninformed opinions.*

I'm so glad that I ignored his narrow-viewed advice. My life has been so much more of a joyful adventure than merely playing it safe. His constant refrain is "survival." I've replied, "That's not enough. I want to thrive!"

Do you have someone close to you who simply does not support your vision?

Walt Disney's own wife, brother/business partner and board of directors were all against Disneyland. Why? There had never been a theme park before. In fact, Walt's wife Lillian asked Walt, "Why do you want to do an amusement park? They're so dirty." Walt replied, "Mine will be clean!"

Walt measured things by his own heart. In fact his first thoughts about creating an amusement park began in 1911 when as a child, he and his sister would stand outside the gates of a Kansas City amusement park. Finally in 1955, Walt opened *his own gates* of Disneyland. Can you hold on to an idea for 44 years? Will you take the steady steps necessary to move forward?

Novelist Greg Bear told me that it took 10 years for readers to discover one of his novels.

My point is that some dreams take several years—and several starts and stops and moments or months of discouragement.

Plenty of people, often those closest to us, will express their doubt. As emphasized in this section, it's really only natural because you are the one who hears your personal and unique "music."

Nurture yourself and your vision—energize the Law of Being in your life.

Get coaching and continue your efforts to learn more and more. [For more about coaching and to learn a powerful method to perform at your best when in a tough situation, see my new video (just 2 min. 40 secs.) when you go to Youtube.com and type in the words "Tom Marcoux How to Perform at Your Best."

This world needs people who hold to their vision and persist.

Thank you!

2) Improve Your Life and Release Needless Suffering

Would you like to move forward faster and shake off needless suffering? I've learned that often facing the truth may hurt in the short run but it eliminates a LOT of suffering. The Law of Being invites us to pay attention to releasing needless suffering.

We'll use the A.I.M. process:

A – arrange space to feel and assess the information

I – intensify your support

M – measure your new behaviors

1. Arrange space to feel and assess the information

A number of people keep themselves too busy to actually feel their feelings.

If you have a big decision to make, schedule some time. If possible, do make time to "sleep on it." You will likely have new thoughts and feelings upon waking up the next day.

Also assess the state of being in the person offering you advice.

Ask these questions in your own mind:

- Does this person really care about my well-being?

- Is this person operating out of fear?
- Is this person (even a family member) blinded by personal needs and fears? Does he or she have my well-being as central to his or her perceptions?

Often, what people say indicates THEIR story and not a focus on your journey.

Be careful.

Rest up.

Make space to refresh yourself so you can see more clearly.

2. Intensify your support

Facing the truth can be really painful and it may drain a lot of your energy. You might even fill up with fear.

The solution is to intensify the support you feel in your daily life.

My clients have . . .
- engaged a therapist
- joined a support group
- talked with a trusted family member or friend
- asked for help around the house in order to recover some personal energy

3. Measure your new behaviors

How do you know if you're really facing the truth? The answer is in your new actions. At one point, I saw that I was getting heavier than I preferred. How did I know that I was facing the truth? I logged my *increase* in daily exercise. I added more time on a treadmill and even raised the amount of weights I use in strength training.

The truth means a lot to me*.

* * *

Remember, when you face the truth, you can ultimately move forward faster and alleviate much needless suffering.

Use these methods:

A – arrange space to feel and assess the information
I – intensify your support
M – measure your new behaviors

Face the truth. Release yourself from needless suffering. Become stronger.

Your experience of life will improve!

3) Find Your OWN Path to Big Success and Lasting Happiness

What do you rest your identity on? In other words: Who are you? And how do you feel about yourself?

As a feature film director, I've worked with classically attractive actors and models. Were they happy? Some of them. Others were on edge. You could see it in their eyes. It was as if their running monologue in their mind was: "If I'm not beautiful [handsome], what am I? Oh, hell! Another wrinkle! Another age spot!"

I invite you to *choose* the essence of your identity in ways that *empower* you. We'll use the O.N. process

O – organize your thoughts and beliefs
N – nullify the "seek approval trap"

---

*I even wrote a book entitled: *Truth No One Will Tell You: How to Feed Your Soul, Save a Business, or Get a Job During an Economic Crisis.*

1. Organize your thoughts and beliefs

Who do you think you are? What is good about you?

A number people define themselves by their roles: good parent, good spouse, good friend.

But there can be a problem here. What? How do you define any of the above roles? Do you define it by what *other* people say?

What if you make the right decision and curb the spending of your spouse, but your spouse gets angry? Some of us would feel bad. Some of us would even think: "If I was a better spouse, I'd make more money and I could get what my sweetie wants."

Really? Is that even true? Are more material things the solution?

I suggest you think of about three different elements as you consider the foundation for your identity: a) your values, b) "your being" and c) your actions.

Let's start with your actions. If you base your whole identity on what you do (say, your job), who are you when you're not doing that? By this, I mean let's avoid having your job be your complete identity. Why? Think about it. Who can a workaholic be if he loses his job? It's likely that he turns desperate and perhaps, depressed. With the job gone, his identity is gone.

So this observation leads us to also include two other elements for the foundation of our identity. *Let's focus on your values.* What is most important to you? I value being helpful to my graduate students/college students, my friends, my family, my clients and my readers. My personal mission is: "I help people experience enthusiasm, love and wisdom to fulfill big dreams." I value expressing my creativity.

Now it's your turn. Pull out a sheet of paper and write

down what you value the most. Next, add "Things I do that support what I value." And note: "New actions I can take to support my values."

Finally, *let's talk about "your being."* Some years ago, my father said, "Do you duty." I replied, "I do my duty and it's not making me happy." The point here is that if you just aim to be a "human doing" instead of a human being, you most likely feel empty inside. How can that be?

A sense of well-being comes from more than mere achievements.

Imagine that "your being" comes from your "being present in this moment." It's not just about finishing some project and then you feel good. Take it from a guy who's directed feature films and published 25 books: Completing projects is enjoyable. However, I spend most of my time "in the process." So it's good to *stay in the present moment* and find meaning in this present moment.

You can be kind in this present moment. You can be creative. You can be loving. You can enjoy laughter. You can hug a loved one. *Be in this present moment.* (That's energizing the Law of Being.)

Also, schedule time to connect with that part of you that experiences calm and peace. For some of us, that's during prayer-time or quiet-time. Some of us only feel a few moments of comfort as we get into a hot bath. Whatever it is for you, connect with those moments. Engage those activities that allow calm and peace into your life. *Be* in the moment with them and the Law of Being will in turn *bless your life.*

2. Nullify the "seek approval trap"

Some of us set up our identity based on someone's approval. It's a trap!

Why? Some people will never give you approval. It helps

to let that go. One of my friends is a snob, and he had disparaging words for one of my books. Fine. I did NOT write that book for him. I let his words go. I'm not seeking his approval.

The secret of leadership is simple: Do what you believe in. Paint a picture of the future. Go there. People will follow. – Seth Godin (in his book Tribes*)*

Many people can tell you about how "no matter what I try, my parent never thinks I'm good enough."

For example, my client "Ellie" endures the burden of dealing with her bitter, judgmental mother.

"You're wrong!" her mother yelled.

Ellie found her voice and replied, "No. I'm different." Ellie learned to find other people who appreciated her as she is. She also learned to value herself on her own terms.

Instead of putting the control of your life into *someone else's hands*, consider making your own choices. Identify your own personal standards.

Don't merely concentrate on getting your preferred results. I've learned that hoping for "perfect audience reactions" can be quite disappointing. Take action and find your meaning in the action. You want to be a kind person—act in kind ways. You want to be a courageous person—take appropriate risks.

Today, I read parts of a book I wrote back in 1989. Ouch. I write better today. And I celebrate that! I celebrate that I had the courage to write my first book back in 1989.

I celebrate that I've written more than 1 million words. I have improved in my craft over the years.

So drop the "need for approval trap." Practice *your* craft. Learn as you go.

Here's how you find your OWN path for big success and lasting happiness: **Develop your OWN criteria for your**

identity. Drop seeking approval to validate yourself.

Instead, empower your own foundation of your identity. Choose your values well, choose "your being," and choose your actions.

BOOK SIX:
YOUR SPRINGBOARD TO STRENGTH AND SUCCESS

In 1989, I had the courage to write my first book. Now, after writing 25 books, I see how my writing style has changed a lot!

Still, I retain interest in five topics that I wrote more than 25 years go. Now in this book, I'm glad to be helpful to you as I revisit and expand upon these topics.

In this section, I'll share insights and methods related to:

1) Courage
2) Destiny
3) Circle of Success (teamwork and networking)
4) Carry on (stay emotionally strong)
5) Replace a Bad Habit with a Good One

Here's How these 5 Topics Relate to the Law of Attraction

1) Courage

You make yourself more attractive when you step forward toward your dreams even if you feel fear. It's as if the universe responds with: "Oh, you *are* serious. You are in motion. Here are more helpful people, resources and opportunities."

2) Destiny

Through the Law of Attraction, the universe wants to help you express your destiny. Many of us feel that destiny is God-given. When you take action, you're saying with a resounding "yes!" that you want to attract more positive elements in helping you fulfill your destiny. As a result of this, you will also feel happier on a daily basis.

3) Circle of Success (teamwork and networking)

It's true—we're all in this together. Every successful person, when speaking candidly, acknowledges that their rise was facilitated by their good and healthy relationships. When you have such good relationships, the Law of Attraction helps you attract more helpful and positive people.

4) Carry on (stay emotionally strong)

The Law of Attraction will often bring us wonderful people and opportunities, but losses do happen regardless of how well things are going. So as we move forward, it is important that we grieve the losses. It is natural and healthy, and grieving is absolutely appropriate because we've lost valuable people and things in our lives. However, we need to learn to grieve *and* still step into each moment fresh. When we do that the Law of Attraction can function well in our lives.

5) Replace a Bad Habit with a Good One

I've learned that simply stopping a bad habit leaves a big hole in our behaviors. That is, we have a hole in a particular "Behavior Sequence." With such a hole, the easiest thing is for the bad habit to return!

To keep to a better path, it helps to *Replace a Bad Habit with a Good One* and eliminate that hole in our behaviors.

Here's the truth: Good habits make us attractive. Why? Because we are perceived as trustworthy. Make good habits happen in your life and the Law of Attraction will bring your more positive people, resources and opportunities.

Let's begin . . .

1. Courage

I learned that courage was not the absence of fear, but the triumph over it. The brave man is not he who does not feel afraid, but he who conquers that fear. - Nelson Mandela

My father could not get himself to go into the operating room. My mother would soon be under local anesthetic, and the doctor would remove a lump from her left breast.

I did not want to see my mother cut open, but I wanted my mother to be comforted during the procedure.

I had no idea what would happen. Would I vomit into my mask? I was afraid. But I willed myself to do what was needed to be done and donned a surgeon's mask.

I sat down next to my mother.

I looked at the wall when the surgeon cut into her.

My mother gripped my hand hard. I saw pain in her eyes. I spoke up, "She's in pain My mother needs more anesthetic."

I thanked the surgical team after my mother received a greater amount of the anesthetic drug. I was glad that I had been in the operating room to help my mother.

What is courage? Merriam-Webster.com defines *courage* as "the ability to do something that you know is difficult or dangerous . . . mental or moral strength to venture, persevere, and withstand danger, fear, or difficulty."

For me, I take action with courage after I've made a decision for a higher value and move forward in spite of fear.

We can develop the habits of courage.

We'll use the C.A.N. process:

C – concentrate energy

A – adapt fear to something usable

N – nurture rehearsal

1) Concentrate energy

Courage is resistance to fear, mastery of fear, not absence of fear. - Mark Twain

How do you master fear? You concentrate your attention on what gets you into action.

Courage is not the absence of fear but rather the judgment that something is more important than fear. – Meg Cabot

I've learned that I can concentrate my energy and focus on what I want in my deepest heart. So for me, **want-power becomes stronger than my fear.**

I asked my sweetheart to describe me and she said, "Hardworking, loving, courageous . . ." The truth is: I face fear a number of times every year.

How do I get myself to face fear? — I *want* big things. I want to fulfill my personal mission: *"I help people experience enthusiasm, love and wisdom to fulfill big dreams."*

I want my three franchises *Jack AngelSword*, *Crystal Pegasus* and *TimePulse* to serve millions of people so well that The Walt Disney Company will want to buy my company near the end of my lifespan. That is, I want my work to serve millions of people beyond my lifespan.

With these "Big Wants," I concentrate my focus and energy. I have the personal energy that is "bigger" than fear.

Beyond my aspirations for The Walt Disney Company to carry on my legacy, and I have goals embodied in my company's mission:

We create energizing, encouraging edutainment for our good and humankind's rise.

– Tom Marcoux Media, LLC Mission Statement

I invite you to write down your Big Wants in your personal journal. Really invest some time to find out what your Big Wants are so they can be stronger than any fear you might feel.

2) Adapt fear to something usable

Several years ago, I wrote in one of my books: "Fear keeps

you on the mountain because fear gets you to prepare."

Make fear your catalyst for preparation.

One again, I emphasize the phrase "ALF – adapt, learn, flex." This relates to courage in that you're not trying to feel comfortable. You're not looking to have the absence of fear. Instead you are using fear to help you put in appropriate time and effort to preparation.

In creativity, everything is a risk. It's not a science . . . You're constantly taking chances. You're constantly taking risks, and you're bound to experience failure. I think one of the critical characteristics or attributes of the leader of a creative business is the ability to tolerate failure. Because it's inevitable. It's bound to happen. There's no such thing as perfection at least over a long period of time in creativity. - Bob Iger, Chairman and CEO, The Walt Disney Company

Bob Iger took a big risk in trying to convince Steve Jobs to sell Pixar to The Walt Disney Company. We're talking about an acquisition for the price of $7.4 billion. What if Pixar faltered? What if there top people quit or passed away?

Over the recent years, the wisdom in Bob Iger's courageous efforts has become clear.

The CEOs of companies that need to grow or need to evolve cannot be risk averse, so while I'm always aware that there's risk involved in some of these big decisions, I focus far more on opportunity. And it was the opportunity that [acquiring] Pixar presented. – Bob Iger

Before any effective leader makes a big move, they get clear in themselves and also make sure to do due diligence. They investigate the crucial details.

Still no one can have all of the data that he or she prefers. You need to step forward in spite of fear.

We get paid by the value we bring to the marketplace.
- Jim Rohn

Success is something you attract by becoming an attractive person. - Jim Rohn

In this book we have been talking about the Law of Attraction. Simply put, when you demonstrate courage, you become more attractive. People can trust that you will take action even though a different person could be paralyzed by fear.

Each person's income is determined primarily by their philosophy. - Jim Rohn

I invite you to have the philosophy to strengthen yourself and use fear as a catalyst for making the best decisions possible.

3) Nurture rehearsal

I emphasize with both college students and clients: "Courage is easier when you're prepared." A cornerstone of preparation is rehearsal.

In fact, to make the value of rehearsal memorable, I have my college students visualize a kindly grandmother saying, "Feeling fear? Rehearse my dear."

Everything valuable in my life has required rehearsal. I've rehearsed before giving a speech or negotiating a deal. I've rehearsed before going to a networking event and before my first day of directing a feature film.

Here's an important insight: **With rehearsal, you actually "exercise your muscles" so you can improvise more effectively on the day of an event.**

In preparing for battle I have always found that plans are useless, but planning is indispensable.

- Dwight D. Eisenhower, 5 Star General and 34th President of the United States of America

Making a plan is like rehearsing the strategic thinking you need to make big things happen.

In summary, to act courageously, condition yourself by making a plan, rehearsing and strengthening yourself.

Principle
Make fear your catalyst for preparation.

Power Questions
How can you prepare? What kind of coaching and rehearsal can help you?

2) Destiny

The only person you are destined to become is the person you decide to be. - Ralph Waldo Emerson

Several years ago, I had a deal to produce a music album for a band I served as both lead singer and song writer.

I had a $1,000 advance in my pocket which was a lot for a college student working his way through college.

But then someone tied with the money started pushing team members around. My intuition told me that this behavior was going to get worse. Further, with this tyrant's pushing his opinion, I saw that great ideas from one of my most creative collaborators getting slapped down. The music album would likely fail.

I gave back the $1,000 plus I had to cover a $1,000 advance that my other band mate had already spent on his keyboard.

It was scary to have to pay the extra $1,000 and to give up the opportunity to produce an album. I did not know what was next for my life.

Soon after I let go of that music industry adventure, I produced and directed my first feature film.

Destiny is a name often given in retrospect to choices that had dramatic consequences. — J.K. Rowling

So I made a big, tough decision to let go of the music album, and my life took an amazing turn.

What destiny would you like for your life?

We'll use the L.I.V.E. process:

L - learn

I - intensify

V - verify

E - experiment

1) Learn

To do something extraordinary, we often need to travel a road quite different from the path of friends or family.

To fulfill your destiny focus on these actions:
- Learn new things
- Learn what really moves your own heart.

I've learned that trying to gain another person's approval can prove truly fruitless. That's why I emphasize *learning what really moves your own heart.*

Some of us say, "I know what I want." That may be so, but many of us have witnessed our priorities and desires change over the years.

Have you noticed that much of our experience is fluid? For example, several years ago I used to eat a lot of Chinese food. Having a girlfriend from Taiwan meant that she, her family and I were in Chinese restaurants every weekend. After nearly eight years of dining on Chinese food in three prominent areas of San Francisco, I developed an allergy to the common food additive MSG. I went to three different restaurants in San Francisco's Chinatown and suffered terrible headaches. I learned that my body chemistry had changed and could no longer tolerate MSG.

I invite you to pay attention and find out what moves your heart *right now.* You may have changed. You can use this knowledge and feeling to empower you to action in fulfilling your destiny.

Big plans and a destiny that make an impact requires one to grow, learn and get coaching.

Nothing is born into this world without labor. – Rob Liano

Everyone needs a coach. It doesn't matter whether you're a basketball player, a tennis player, a gymnast or a bridge player.
- Bill Gates

Finally, learn what patterns to set so that you consistently take action (elsewhere in this book I share the *Trigger-Set Method*). For example, I know that I have a daily habit of reading. I can use that habit to *trigger* getting some exercise. *I read for 35 minutes while walking briskly on a treadmill.* I learned to take advantage of my reading habit by making sure I exercise daily.

What habit or tendency can *you* learn to use for fulfilling your own destiny?

2) Intensify

To experience a truly fulfilling life, we often need to intensify our efforts. That is, turn away from mind-numbing activities, and devote ourselves to that which causes our destiny to blossom.

For example, it's a Saturday night, and after returning from an event with friends, I'm back at the keyboard. Why? *The way to get better at one's art form is to practice it.* I write everyday. I also find that improving one's technique can often bring some joy to the day.

The fault, dear Brutus, is not in our stars but in ourselves."
— *William Shakespeare (the play,* Julius Caesar)

The idea of destiny being in our hands does not sit well with a number of people. For example, I've paid close attention while I continue teach Comparative Religion on the college level (for over 12 years). Numerous people report that they believe *God set their destiny* and that they get hints during prayer or meditation. Sounds fine to me.

Here I'm talking about taking such guidance/intuition and then intensifying your personal efforts. We can view the word "intensify" as increasing our personal efforts to *"live our destiny."*

For example, Jack Canfield and Mark Victor Hansen developed their "five actions of promotion everyday" pattern. Everyday, Jack and Mark would be on radio talk shows, giving speeches, appearing on TV shows and more to promote their book *Chicken Soup for the Soul*. That's ten actions per day. You know that has to add up!

Those actions led to more than 250 titles in the *Chicken Soup for the Soul* series with around 500 million books sold!

Don't worry about failures, worry about the chances you miss when you don't even try. – Jack Canfield

Everything you want is on the other side of fear. – Jack Canfield

Everything you want is out there waiting for you to ask. Everything you want also wants you. But you have to take action to get it. – Jack Canfield

To really fulfill your destiny, take lots of action.

3) Verify

Letting go means to come to the realization that some people are a part of your history, but not a part of your destiny.

- Steve Maraboli

To live well and fulfill your destiny, you need to face the truth. Sometimes the people we long to have support us simply do *not* want to or do *not* have the capacity to truly support us.

Observe closely. *Verify* if someone is building you up or actually tearing you down.

Surround yourself with only people who are going to lift you higher. – Oprah Winfrey

Some of my clients choose **to protect their personal health and energy** by *minimizing* the time they spend with family members who cut them down with mean and cruel comments.

Another area to verify is *measuring your results that you are getting with your current actions*. One of my clients, with my guidance, realized that she needed to turn from just writing books to making videos. Why? Many people in her target audience will never read books. To serve those people, a video is a much better match.

My point is: Verify what is working and what is not working. Then adjust your plan and your actions.

4) Experiment

All life is an experiment. The more experiments you make the better. - Ralph Waldo Emerson

Let me share with you the journey of someone I admire — a dear friend.

Here's her journey so far:
- Trained as a hair stylist
- Owned multiple hair salons
- Sold her business and traveled the world
- Earned a degree in graphic design
- Did graphic design work, helping a church
- Earned a certification at the California Culinary Academy
- Cooked with George Lucas' private chef
- Cooked, serving the artists at Pixar
- Wrote books that sell consistently on Amazon.com
- Currently completing a children's book

I'm impressed with the breadth of adventures she has had. What an interesting and fulfilling life!

I would say, as an entrepreneur everything you do—every action you take in product development, in marketing, every conversation you have, everything you do—is an experiment. If you can conceptualize your work not as building features, not as launching campaigns, but as running experiments, you can get radically more done with less effort. – Eric Ries

Here's something I want to truly emphasize:

It's by experimenting and taking appropriate risks that you find what really brings you joy.

You'll likely find that you'll enjoy different things in different chapters of your life.

Here are *some* of my experiments:
- operations analyst (part of the team that put the first bank into online banking)
- screenwriter, feature film director/producer (won a special award at the Emmy Awards)
- Guest Instructor to Stanford University MBA students
- author of 25 books
- creator and art director of a trilogy of *Jack AngelSword* graphic novels
- (elsewhere I mentioned lead singer/song writer, actor in feature films and commercials, model)

I include the above *to share with you that I speak from experience* and not just theory. I've learned that happiness—that is, day to day happiness—is not a panacea that you arrive at and stay there for the rest of your life. Instead, many of us need new challenges and new vistas.

I've learned you can do a job-for-the-rent and your art work—during the same week. In fact, as an artist/author/filmmaker, I've learned that my "regular life" informs and deepens my art.

If you're going to invent, it means you're going to experiment, and if you're going to experiment, you're going to fail, and if you're going to fail, you have to think long term. - Jeff Bezos

Experiment, get coaching, build up your skills, try new things and Be Seen Doing Good Work. In these ways, you expand the opportunities rushing to you.

* * *

Often, I say to my graduate students and college students, "This material is like a buffet table. Take what you like and leave the rest."

My point is: If you feel that your destiny is God-given, go forward and explore and see what blessings and talents you have. Consider meditating or praying to get access to intuition and Divine guidance.

In my 1989 book, I wrote: "Destiny is like a pool of water. You dive in and are refreshed. You need to dive in again and again in different ways."

So consider using the L.I.V.E. process: "Learn, Intensify, Verify and Experiment."

Living your destiny will give you great highs and some tough lows . . . and it's worth it! Good journey to you.

Principle
You discover and fulfill your destiny by experimenting and taking appropriate risks.

Power Questions
How can you devote more time, energy and effort to

finding and fulfilling your destiny? What experiments and coaching would help you?

3. Circle of Success (teamwork and networking)

Sometimes, idealistic people are put off the whole business of networking as something tainted by flattery and the pursuit of selfish advantage. But virtue in obscurity is rewarded only in Heaven. To succeed in this world you have to be known to people.

- Sonia Sotomayor, the Supreme Court's First Latina Justice

At the airport, I turned to my co-producer and cameraman and said the next shot was for the American Eagle airplane to roar down the runway with the two main characters running after it. The fact that I had the plane and San Luis Obispo airport for free in my first feature film was a testament to what I call the Circle of Success.

To have this good fortune was the result of my actions two years before. I wrote a screenplay that took an unusual path:
- I gave the screenplay to a software engineer
- He passed it to another software engineer
- She passed it to a real estate developer
- He passed it to the California Motion Picture Commissioner.

The California Motion Picture Commissioner arranged for the free use of San Luis Obispo Airport and the American Eagle airplane.

Some time later, through social media, a Washington D.C. attorney connected with me. I helped him by sharing good ideas about marketing through social media. In turn, he connected me with an attorney I was looking to find on the West Coast of the United States. He connected me with the chairperson of the entertainment division of a 400 person law firm in the heart of Los Angeles, California.

I remember this quote that applies to the Circle of Success idea:

Nothing is impossible for the man who doesn't have to do it himself. - A. H. Weiler

To help you develop an effective network of contacts we'll use the A.I.M. process:

A – arrange your great personal brand
I – intensify "help them first"
M – magnify the good

1) Arrange your great personal brand

Your personal brand is the answer to the question: "What are you best known for?"

When you want to go further faster, you'll take good care to have an effective personal brand. You want to be known as someone who is both competent and caring.

I guide my college students to use this mnemonic device for developing an extraordinary personal brand: T.H.O.R. (trustworthy, helpful, organized, respectful).

In a sea of unbelievable choice, relentless choice, I do think that you have some advantage, if you've got a good brand. - Bob Iger, Chairman and CEO, The Walt Disney Company

In many ways, a personal brand is a promise of performance. People trust that you will do what you say you will do.

Personal branding is about managing your name—even if you don't own a business—in a world of misinformation, disinformation, and semi-permanent Google records. Going on a date? Chances are that your "blind" date has Googled your name. Going to a job interview? Ditto. – Tim Ferriss

Be sure to do those actions that build your great personal brand including: a) return phone calls/emails quickly, b) take care with your promises, c) if something changes, alert people involved quickly, and d) demonstrate that you can learn from your mistakes.

Finally, make sure that people know that you're coachable. Show that you have your ego in check and that you seek to learn from every situation.

2) Intensify "help them first"

"The 3 Magic Words of Networking are 'Help Them First.'" I shared this with my college students in one of my Designing Careers classes.

I explained that many of us may feel reluctant or embarrassed about asking for help from the people in our circle of contacts. However, if you have *already* been helpful to someone, that person is likely to want to reciprocate and help you in return.

Here are examples of Helping Them First:

1) Listen to them

2) Buy their book (if they're having a book signing)

3) Ask them a question that helps them say what they want (if they're giving a speech or leading a meeting). Such a question might be: "What one thing do you want us to remember most about this?"

4) Send them resources (perhaps, you send a link to a helpful article).

It's a Circle of Success. We rise together. – Tom Marcoux

The above phrase is one that I wrote for my 1989 book. It's fun to bring it back for this book in your hand. In your Circle of Success, you're really developing business friendships. It's true that there are different levels of friendship. Some people you only trust to talk about a shared hobby and then a certain few people you may talk about heartfelt subjects.

In any case, your target is to develop healthy, positive interactions with several people—your Circle of Success.

Networking is not about just connecting people. It's about connecting people with people, people with ideas, and people with opportunities. - Michele Jennae

For many of us, the Circle of Success idea also applies to teamwork.

Give a good idea to a mediocre team, and they will screw it up. Give a mediocre idea to a great team, and they will either fix it or come up with something better. If you get the team right, chances are that they'll get the ideas right. – Ed Catmull, President of Pixar and Disney Animation.

I have led teams since I directed my first short film at the age of 9. I've learned that leadership is a topic that deserves study and practice. Leadership really begins with *self-leadership*.

Here are some questions that can help guide you to be a better team leader.

Can team members . . .

- Count on me for prompt feedback?
- Rely on me to see the *good* that they are accomplishing?
- Count on me to find out where I'm holding the team back and to correct my own behavior?
- Trust me to make the hard decisions and serve the team?
- Count on me to take care of myself and stay strong?
- Rely on me to make the right decision even if some people's feelings may be bothered?
- Count on me to remove negative influences (including disruptive people) when necessary?
- Trust me to be strong enough to hear the truth?

Also, a leader must find team members who are flexible, competent, caring, trustworthy—and who show initiative.

Developing your network and team require constant vigilance.

3) Magnify the good

My mentor Dottie Walters shared with me a good detail to place into a conversation. Tell the other person, "Oh. That tells me something about you." Then provide a specific and sincere compliment.

No matter how busy you are, you must take time to make the other person feel important. - Mary Kay Ash

Pretend that every single person you meet has a sign around his or her neck that says, "Make me feel important." Not only will you succeed in sales, you will succeed in life. - Mary Kay Ash

Many of us spend most of our time "putting out fires" and that leaves little time to magnify the good.

We need to set a pattern in which we are telling people specifically what they've done well and how much we appreciate their efforts.

Sharon Lechter, author of *Think and Grow Rich for Women*, recommends her personal system of "2-2-2." Each day she writes 2 emails, 2 posts on social media and 2 handwritten notes.

When you praise people specifically and sincerely in many of the elements of "2-2-2," you can build up your personal network and team.

I would add another "2" to Sharon's "2-2-2." Add two phone calls in which you're catching up with someone and listening closely. You can begin a conversation with: "Is this a good time to talk? (The person says, "Yes.") How are things going for you?"

Phone calls can be better because you can put warmth in your voice.

Be sure to devote good energy and efforts to your Circle

of Success.

Principle
Help them first—and strengthen your network.

Power Questions
Who do you want to connect with? How can you help them first?

4. Carry on (stay emotionally strong)

Our greatest glory is not in never failing, but in rising up every time we fail. – Ralph Waldo Emerson

To make the most of your life, you'll need to carry on even when you feel emotionally torn apart. Many of us have dreams that take much effort and a significant amount of time.

I believed it [that I would succeed], but it took longer."
– Vanessa Williams, singer, actress, star of Broadway, Film and Television

You may believe that you have talent and maybe even a God-given destiny to fulfill. *And*, you'll need to stay strong and moving forward even when you've suffered significant defeat.

We need to learn to grieve *and* still step into each moment fresh. When we do that the Law of Attraction can function well in our lives.

A professional is someone who can do his best work when he doesn't feel like it. - Alistair Cooke

I've learned that it helps to condition yourself to do certain actions regardless of your mood. This helps you succeed.

There are two types of pain you will go through in life, the pain of discipline and the pain of regret. Discipline weighs ounces while regret weighs tons. - Jim Rohn

To develop useful disciplines that help you carry on, we'll use the O.N.E. process:

O – open to an Empowering Thought

N – nurture your Low Mood First Aid Kid

E – engage purposeful conditioning

(I chose the word "One" in the spirit of one of the meanings of *integrity* "the state of being complete or whole." Merriam-Webster.com)

1) Open to an Empowering Thought

Sow a thought and you reap an action; sow an act and you reap a habit; sow a habit and you reap a character; sow a character and you reap a destiny. – Ralph Waldo Emerson

Fear may arise and some things may go wrong. It's hard to do the most important thing when your emotions are swirling like a tornado. I've learned a useful habit that helps me stay productive.

My dad told me, "It takes fifteen years to be an overnight success," and it took me seventeen and a half years.

- Adrien Brody, Oscar-winning actor

I trained myself to *add an Empowering Thought of "I'm not done yet."* A couple of weeks before I turned 30, I felt bad. I looked around and I was nowhere near where I wanted to be by that age. Then I devised a practice that helped me for years. I decided to do a ceremony that celebrated where I was at the time. I wrote down the positive things I was "doing now." In this way I gave myself credit for the action I was taking on a daily basis. Then I gathered, for my birthday, my inner circle of friends and I "launched" my *List of Doing Now* like I was launching a ship. I used a paper tube filled with confetti instead of a bottle (that one smashes on the side of a ship), but nonetheless, I was christening the moment.

In essence this practice of *Celebrating the Doing Now*, turned my thoughts to what *I was grateful* to be doing and what I did with positive feeling. I focused on what I was building and **NOT** on where I had not arrived.

This practice of *adding an Empowering Thought* continues in my verbal habits. For example, when someone asks me whether I know a particular top person in the film industry and I haven't encountered the person, *I reply: "Not yet."* Implied in my response is my hopeful focus that I'm continuing to expand my contacts everyday (which is true).

What Empowering Thought can you add to your habitual thoughts? This is really about conditioning yourself to think in an empowering manner.

For example, over the years, when I was doing a job that merely helped me to pay my rent, I'd add an Empowering Thought. If I complained about a new procedure, *I immediately added, "I'm grateful for steady work."*

Upon saying that phrase, I found myself feeling better.

Now, I invite you to write down Empowering Thoughts of your own. What ideas have actually changed the direction of your thinking? I call such an idea a "SwitchPhrase" because it functions like a switch at a railroad yard. The switch shifts the train to another track. Another way to say this is: "This is a shift in the direction of a train-of-thought."

My clients have shared these "SwitchPhrases:"
- I know it!—I'm on the right track—my success is building everyday.
- I now know what doesn't work—I'll adapt—I'll do better with my next effort.
- I'm okay right now.
- Each day, I'm taking a step. I'm building a better

life for my family.

Pick your own Empowering Thoughts and memorize them.

2) Nurture your Low Mood First Aid Kid

A number of people talk about the importance of taking the appropriate risk.

The person who risks nothing does nothing, has nothing, is nothing, and becomes nothing. He may avoid suffering and sorrow, but he simply cannot learn and feel and change and grow and love and live. – Leo F. Buscaglia

If you give up on your dreams, what's left? – Jim Carrey

There's something liberating about not pretending. Dare to embarrass yourself. Risk. – Drew Barrymore

Taking an appropriate risk is crucial to fulfilling your destiny and enjoying a happy life. However, *you need the energy and strength to take the risks!*

Here's how to build up your energy especially when you feel bad or are in a "low mood":

Nurture your Low Mood First Aid Kid.

The word "nurture" means "to help (something or someone) to grow, develop, or succeed" [Merriam-Webster.com].

The idea is to develop your list of what helps you shift to a stronger state of being when you're in a Low Mood.

We're talking about comforting yourself *and* shifting to an Empowered state of being—when you can.

My clients have included the following on their lists ("Low Mood First Aid Kit"):
- listen to soothing music
- take a walk
- call a kind friend
- take a hot bath

- escape to my car and listen to music with the doors locked and my eyes closed
- walk in nature (at least at the park)
- walk near water
- see a sad movie and have a good cry
- go for a run

On a number of occasions, I listen to music and assemble a puzzle. That's a peaceful time in my day.

Carry your list and related items with you. It can be a simple as carrying an iPod, preprogrammed with empowering playlists of music. Take good care of yourself.

3) Engage purposeful conditioning

If you don't program yourself, life will program you!
- Les Brown

Your real power is in your making choices about your own programming. What do you read or watch on TV everyday? Do have any moments of the day when you purposely place positive, uplifting ideas and messages into your own mind?

I celebrate that you're reading this book. It can serve you to build up your own purposeful conditioning.

Conditioning is defined as "a simple form of learning involving the formation, strengthening, or weakening of an association between a stimulus and a response" (Merriam-webster.com).

The idea is to program yourself so that when a certain stimulus happens, you have an empowered response.

Here's an example: Several years ago, after running with my father, I'd get an ice cream cone. Not a good plan! Calories were used up by running and immediately replaced by ice cream.

I had conditioned myself to expect a reward of ice cream.

In recent years after exercising, I now turn to oranges. That's making a good decision about my conditioning.

Realize that it's crucial that you use your own mind in empowering ways.

Happiness comes from within. It is not dependent on external things or on other people. You become vulnerable and can be easily hurt when your feelings of security and happiness depend on the behavior and actions of other people. Never give your power to anyone else. - Brian L. Weiss

Purposeful conditioning includes making a choice to do what's necessary in order to strengthen yourself.

For example, *one way to condition yourself is to read and talk about how top people think and take action.*

Recently, I talked with a friend "Tucker." I told him the story of how Steve Jobs made a bold move to take Pixar public (as a publicly traded company) when only the first film *Toy Story* had been released. Other Pixar people thought it best to wait until Pixar had more than one successful film.

Steve said, "No. This is Pixar's moment," and he said, "We do it now [because as soon as *Toy Story* comes out Disney CEO Michael] Eisner will attempt to change the deal between Disney and Pixar."

So Steve went through with the plan and like clockwork Michael Eisner attempted to change the deal with Pixar. But due to Steve's prescient plan, Pixar was now a public company worth so much that the renegotiation ended in Pixar's favor with a new 50-50 split of proceeds from their films.

My friend Tucker's response was: "Well, he could do that. He has a lot of money. He could take a risk."

On the other hand, I thought (to myself): "That's probably one of the reasons that Tucker is stuck. Instead of studying how to make audacious moves, Tucker just writes off the courage, due diligence and bold moves of successful people."

Unfortunately, Tucker is *not* purposefully conditioning himself to see opportunity, strengthen his own resolve and then take appropriate risks.

Again, one way to purposefully condition yourself is to study the mindset and moves of top successful people. Tell these stories and see how you can apply their lessons learned to your own journey.

I always tell my kids if you lay down, people will step over you. But if you keep scrambling, if you keep going, someone will always, always give you a hand. Always. But you gotta keep dancing, you gotta keep your feet moving. - Morgan Freeman

You simply have to put one foot in front of the other and keep going. Put blinders on and plow right ahead. - George Lucas

The way to carry on is to live and breathe the empowering stories of people who stretched, took appropriate risks and made bold moves.

If you want better in your life, you'll need to do *new* actions.

Principle

To carry on, be sure to make good choices about your own conditioning.

Power Questions

What can you do on a daily basis to build up your purposeful conditioning? Will you listen to empowering audio programs, read books, and see empowering videos? Who inspires you? Will you read biographies of top successful people?

5. Replace a Bad Habit with a Good One

The difference between an amateur and a professional is in their habits. An amateur has amateur habits. A professional has professional habits. We can never free ourselves from habit. But we can replace bad habits with good ones. - Steven Pressfield

One of the most powerful things I've learned is that getting a bad habit out of your life works well when you *replace the bad habit with a Good One!*

If you only try to cut out a bad habit, you have a hole in your Behavior-Sequence. A Behavior-Sequence begins with a trigger and results in your action. For example, a while ago, I might finish a long day and at 1 AM in the morning, I may want to see some funny video program that I pre-recorded. Now, if I see cookies on the coffee table that's a powerful trigger! I might automatically reach for a cookie which would not help me stay fit and trim.

So in this section, I'll share with you how to be systematic about triggers and replacing a bad habit with a good one.

We'll use the U.P. process:

U – use the Trigger-Set Method

P – prepare when you're "cool"

1) Use the Trigger-Set Method

For years, I have coached clients in the *Trigger-Set Method.*

The first thing to do is to identify the beginning of a Behavior-Sequence which makes up what you deem as a bad habit.

Let's return to my above example about seeing a bag of cookies and being triggered to have one or two.

I've learned that I can set up a *replacement* for a cookie. I can have a cup of water while I'm watching a video.

Or I can set up having oranges on the table instead of the cookies (I can keep the cookies out of sight in the pantry.)

The Trigger-Set Method can be used especially for developing good habits that lead to excellent productivity.

A professional is someone who can do his best work when he doesn't feel like it. - Alistair Cooke

So how can you set a trigger that makes you go immediately to work no matter how you feel?

When I train clients to be more productive, I help them discover their own preferred pattern of Trigger and Empowered Behavior.

One client, Miranda, set up a Binder with her current book project on her nightstand. The first thing she sees in the morning is her *Book-in-Progress Binder.* She picks up the binder and goes over to her desktop and writes for the first 30 minutes of the day before she gets ready to go to her regular job (that pays her bills). In this manner, she writes about 200 words a day. Over 355 days, that adds up to 71,000 words. Miranda's Book-in-Progress Binder serves as her positive trigger. She tells me that printing pages every day and placing them in her binder gives her a tangible feeling of progress.

I also advised her to keep a *Progress Log.* For example, as I type this sentence, I know that my current word count for this book is 55,907 words. This relates to my phrase:

Keep score and achieve more.

The Progress Log helps many of us get past the initial moments of hesitation. Some of us have allowed such moments to spiral down into procrastination.

Instead, using the Progress Log to even write just 200 words a day, can help us simply feel better. We feel proud of ourselves for having the discipline to take even little steps forward.

I don't sing because I'm happy; I'm happy because I sing.
– William James

We must make automatic and habitual, as early as possible, as many useful actions as we can. - William James

The Trigger-Set Method truly focuses on learning to use our brain to our greatest advantage. In this way, we make useful actions habitual.

So what new habits would really turn your life in a better direction?

2) Prepare when you're "cool"

Prepare your Trigger-Sequence while you're cool before a hot situation.

Here's an example. When I'm in the car, on the way back from a restaurant, I announce to my sweetheart, "I'm jumping on the treadmill as soon as I get in the house."

I've just made arriving in the door of my home as the Trigger so that I go straight to the treadmill and begin a 35 minute session on the exercise equipment. There is no hesitation! And indecision is eliminated from the pattern.

There is no more miserable human being than one in whom nothing is habitual but indecision. – William James

The vital distinction that I'm emphasizing here is that you set your Trigger when your emotions are "cool."

It's really tough to "do the right thing" when you're upset. But if you have set the Trigger-Sequence on automatic, you can do the right thing more consistently.

Trust is built with consistency. – Lincoln Chafee

Success is the sum of small efforts, repeated day in and day out. – Robert Collier

My clients use a number of Progress Logs and pre-set Trigger-Sequences to enhance their productivity.

Successful people are simply those with success habits. – Brian Tracy

Principle

Replace a Bad Habit with a Good One—set up a Trigger-Sequence when you're "cool."

Power Questions

What new and better habits do you wish to form? How will your life improve once you're consistently taking action with these new habits? What triggers can you set when you are comfortable and "cool" so that when a situation is hot, *you automatically do take good action?*

* * *

When I recently glanced at my 1989 book, I found that I did *not* want to update it. I still wanted to address the topics, but I also did not feel pulled to write a whole book . . . yet. So I have given myself the opportunity write about the topics and share the above insights with you in *this* book.

Still, I'm glad I wrote that first book because it gave me a chance to hone my craft of writing. Back in 1989, I did *not* allow a close friend at the time to talk me out of my plan to write a book.

I've learned the truth of these two principles:
- Practice your craft.
- We learn by doing.

What do you want to improve in your life? Do you have a particular craft or gift that you want to develop?

Top author Malcolm Gladwell refers to 10,000 hours as being a prerequisite for many professionals to perfect their craft.

Instead of getting stuck and saying, "I don't have a particular area to focus on," take a brief inventory of your life. Pay attention particularly to those things you did because they were intrinsically fun. Perhaps, you'll start to become aware of what you've been "practicing" already.

So you're not starting at 10,000 hours. You may be starting at 5,231 hours to go.

One of my former graduate students said, "25 books. That's a lot, Tom."

I replied, "Well, writing is one of my art forms."

I invite you to start putting time and effort into something that makes you really feel alive. Good journey to you.

A FINAL WORD AND THE SPRINGBOARD TO YOUR DREAMS

Congratulations on your efforts with this book. Thank you for your attention. When you return to these pages again and again, you can *reenergize yourself*. You will get more value each time you review the steps covered in this book.

To gain more value and use this book as a springboard, be sure to go through it and note your new tasks *in your calendar*. Take some action. Any action towards improving skills and enlarging your life is helpful. I often say, "Better than zero."

* * *

Please consider gaining special training through my coaching (phone and in-person), workshops, presentations and Top Five Group Elite Video Training. My coaching features innovations: *Dynamic Rehearsal* and *Power Rehearsal for Crisis*. Due to my background in improvisation and training in acting, directing and screenwriting, I help clients *as I improvise dialogue* during rehearsal sessions. I coach clients to prepare for speeches and any tough or vital conversation with audiences, colleagues, sales prospects and even family members.

As you continue to work toward expanding your financial abundance and fulfillment in life, you are likely to come up against some tough situations. To be supportive I've written a number of books . . .

- Darkest Secrets of Charisma
- Darkest Secrets of Persuasion and Seduction Masters: How to Protect Yourself and Turn the Power to Good

- Darkest Secrets of Negotiation Masters
- Darkest Secrets of Making a Pitch to the Film and Television Industry
- Darkest Secrets of Film Directing
- Darkest Secrets of the Film and Television Industry Every Actor Should Know
- Darkest Secrets of Spiritual Seduction Masters
- Success Secrets of Rich, Smart and Powerful People: How You Can Use Leverage for Business Success

See my blog at
www.BeHeardandBeTrusted.com

The best to you,
Tom
Tom Marcoux,
America's Communication Coach, TFG Thought Leader, Motion Picture Director, Actor, Producer, Screenwriter
P.S. See **Free Chapters** of Tom Marcoux's 25 books at http://amzn.to/ZiCTRj   (at Amazon.com)

Titles include:
Be Heard and Be Trusted
Nothing Can Stop You This Year
Truth No One Will Tell You
10 Seconds to Wealth
Reduce Clutter, Enlarge Your Life
Wake Up Your Spirit to Prosperity   — and more.
(For coaching, reach Tom Marcoux
 at tomsupercoach@gmail.com)

EXCERPT FROM
DARKEST SECRETS OF PERSUASION AND SEDUCTION MASTERS: HOW TO PROTECT YOURSELF AND TURN THE POWER TO GOOD

by Tom Marcoux, America's Communication Coach
Copyright Tom Marcoux

... Now, I am in my 40's, with gray in my hair, and for 27 years I have been taking action to protect people.

And now is the time for me to protect you with the Countermeasures I reveal in this book.

Every human being needs to be able to
break the trance that a Manipulator creates.
You need to make good decisions
so you are safe and you keep growing
—and you are not cut down and crippled.

This Darkest Secrets material is so intense that I first released it only with the counterbalance of my most energizing and uplifting books, Nothing Can Stop You This Year! and 10 Seconds to Wealth: Master the Moment Using Your Divine Gifts.

An interviewer asked me: "Who can be the Manipulator?"

A co-worker, a boss, a salesperson, someone you're dating, and someone you think is a friend.

Now is the time—this very minute—for me to write this book to protect you.

I must speak the truth.

These Darkest Secrets of "persuasion masters" are ...

Wait a minute! Let's say it plainly: These are the Darkest Secrets of masters of manipulation. Throughout this book, I will call these people what they are: Manipulators.

Dictionary.com defines "manipulate" as "To influence or

manage shrewdly or deviously.... To tamper with or falsify for personal gain."

In this book, we will look on a manipulator as one who deviously influences someone with no concern about that person's well-being, and who causes harm to that person.

Here is the first Darkest Secret:

Darkest Secret #1:
Manipulators Make You Hurt
and Then Offer the Salve.

Manipulators would invite you to go out in the sun for hours and then sell you the salve to soothe your burns. The problem is that we don't notice that this is what they're doing.

For example, you're considering the purchase of a house. A Manipulator asks the question, "So, where would you put your TV?" This question is designed to put you into a trance.

Dictionary.com defines "trance" as "a half-conscious state, seemingly between sleeping and waking, in which ability to function voluntarily may be suspended." Let's condense this: in a trance you may not be able to function freely.

Here is the second Secret:

Darkest Secret #2:
Manipulators Put You into a Trance.

To protect yourself, you must learn to use Countermeasures to Break the Trance.

All the Countermeasures (actions you can take to break the trance) in this book will make you stronger and more capable of protecting yourself.

Now, we'll view the third Secret:

Darkest Secret #3:
Manipulators Care Nothing for You and Human
Decency: They'll lie, cheat, and do whatever they need

to do so they win—but their charm masks all this.

Let's return to the example of a Manipulator selling you a house. A Manipulator does not pause for an instant to see if you can truly afford the new house. The Manipulator would neglect to mention that you will not only have your mortgage payment of $900. There will be additional costs: home repairs, property tax, water, electricity, homeowner's insurance, and more. The Manipulator only emphasizes what he or she knows you want to hear: "Look! $900 is better than the $1500 you're paying for rent, which is just going down the toilet. And the $900 is an investment."

Let's go back to **Darkest Secret #1:**

Manipulators make you hurt and then offer the salve.

The Manipulator has you feeling good about the solution (salve) and feeling bad about your current life situation.

How? A Manipulator will make you hurt through questions such as:

• What bothers you about paying $1500 a month for rent? (The Manipulator will use a derisive tone when he says the word rent.)

• What is not smart about paying rent on someone else's house instead of investing in your own house?

• How do you feel about your children walking in the neighborhood where you live now?

Do you see how these questions are designed to make you hurt enough so that you'll buy?

An interviewer asked me, "Tom, aren't these good arguments for purchasing a house?"

"What we're looking at is the *intention* of the influencer," I replied. "Let's look at our definition of a manipulator as one who deviously influences someone with no concern about that person's well-being, and who causes harm to that person. If the person truly cannot afford the house, he or she will be harmed by buying it. If the manipulator conceals the truth, the manipulator is doing harm. That's the important difference."

Some friends of mine are ethical and helpful real estate agents who truthfully reveal the whole situation and help the purchaser achieve her own goals.

In this book, we are talking about another type of person; that is, unethical Manipulators.

* * *

In any given moment, we need to remember the tactics Manipulators use. We will focus on the word D.A.R.K. so you can remember details easily and protect yourself from Manipulators.

D — Dangle something for nothing
A — Alert to scarcity
R — Reveal the Desperate Hot Button
K — Keep on pushing buttons

1. Dangle Something for Nothing

What do conmen and conwomen do to seize your attention? They make you think you're getting a "steal."

I recently saw a documentary in which a conman on a street in England showed a toy that looked like it was dancing. This fake product was actually dancing because of a hidden, invisible thread. The conman was dangling something for nothing. The Entranced Buyer thought he was getting something worth $20 for only $5. That was the trick. The Entranced Buyer felt that he was getting $15 extra of value for his $5. What the Buyer really got was something worth nothing. Similarly, I know someone who purchased a copy of a Disney movie from a street vendor in San

Francisco. She brought the copy home and it was unwatchable—and the street vendor was never seen again.

An old phrase goes, "A conman cannot con someone who is not looking for something for nothing."

How to Protect Yourself from "Dangle Something for Nothing"

Stop! Get on your cell phone and talk through the "deal" with someone you know who thinks clearly. Go home. Think about it. Do some research on the Internet. Listen to your gut feelings. If the salesman or conman is too insistent, get away from that Manipulator. Get quiet. Have a cup of water. Cool down. Break the Trance!

Break the Trance and Identify the Crucial Detail

Earlier, I mentioned that a Manipulator puts you into a trance. An added problem is that we put ourselves into a trance. For example, as you read this, are you thinking about your right toe? Most likely not (unless you stubbed your toe recently). The point is that we only focus on a tiny percentage of what is going on in our life.

Around fifteen years ago, I caused myself trouble because I put myself into a trance. I discovered that under certain conditions, friendship can make you nearly deaf. Here's how: I was producing a song for a motion picture. A good friend was singing backup in the chorus. Because of our friendship, I wanted him to sound great. I completely missed the Crucial Detail. In this kind of situation, the Crucial Detail is that what truly counts is how the lead singer sounds! I made a song that I could not release. What a waste of time and money! I had put myself into a trance.

In any situation in which the Manipulator is "dangling

something for nothing," we often fall into a trance and miss the Crucial Detail. The most important detail is *not* that we're saving money if we order before midnight tonight. What counts is whether the product creates a lasting, crucial benefit in our lives. And is the benefit of the product worth the cost? Some people even program themselves to make mistakes by saying, "I can't pass up a bargain." The bargain is *not* the Crucial Detail.

Secrets to Break the Trance

This is the process of B.R.E.A.K.S. It will help you remember the proven methods to break a trance.

B — Breathe
R — Relax
E — Envision
A — Act on aromas
K — Keep moving
S — Smile

Secret #1: Breathe

Remember Secret #1: Manipulators make you hurt and then offer the salve. The Manipulator wants to put you into a state of being that fills you with a sense of urgency and anxiety. Oh, no! I'm going to miss the sale!

Stop this highly vulnerable state. Take a deep breath. Do it now. Take a deep breath and let your belly "get fat" by filling it with air. As you breathe out, let your belly deflate. Breathe in through your nose and breathe out through your mouth. This is called belly-breathing. Repeat the actions of belly-breathing three times. Good. Now, do you feel different? Remember, when you are relaxed, you are strong.

End of Excerpt from
DARKEST SECRETS OF PERSUASION AND SEDUCTION MASTERS: HOW TO PROTECT YOURSELF AND TURN THE POWER TO GOOD
Copyright Tom Marcoux Media, LLC

Purchase your copy of this book (paperback or ebook) at Amazon.com or BarnesandNoble.com
See **Free Chapters** of Tom Marcoux's 24 books at http://amzn.to/ZiCTRj

ABOUT THE AUTHOR

Tom Marcoux helps people like you fulfill big dreams. Known as America's Communication Coach and TFG Thought Leader, Tom has authored 24 books with sales in 15 countries. One of his *Darkest Secrets* books rose to #1 on Amazon.com Hot New Releases in Business Life (and in Business Communication). He guides clients and audiences (IBM, Sun Microsystems, etc.) to success in job interviewing, public speaking, media relations, and branding. A member of the National Speakers Association, he is a professional coach and guest expert on TV, radio, and print, and was dubbed "the Personal Branding Instructor" by the *San Francisco Examiner*.

Tom addressed National Association of Broadcasters' Conference six years running. With a degree in psychology, Tom is a guest lecturer at **Stanford University**, DeAnza, & California State University, and teaches public speaking, science fiction cinema/literature and comparative religion at Academy of Art University. Winner of a special award at the **Emmys**, Tom wrote, directed, and produced a feature film that the distributor took to the **Cannes film market**, and the film gained international distribution. He is engaged in book/film projects *Crystal Pegasus* (children's) and *TimePulse* (science fiction). See TomSuperCoach.com and Tom's well-received blog
   at www.BeHeardandBeTrusted.com

Tom Marcoux can help you with **speech writing** and **coaching for your best performance.**
   As Tom says, *Make Your Speech a Pleasant Beach.*
   Join Tom's Linkedin.com group: *Executive Public Speaking and Communication Power.*

At Google+: join the community "Create Your Best Life – Charisma & Confidence"

Get a **Free** report: "9 Deadly Mistakes to Avoid for Your Next Speech and 9 Surefire Methods" at
http://tomsupercoach.com/freereport9Mistakes4Speech.html

Tom Marcoux has trained CEOs, small business owners, and graduate students to speak with impact and gain audiences' tremendous approval and cooperation. *Learn how to present and get thunderous applause!*

"Tom, Thanks for your coaching and work with me on revising my speech at a major university. Working with you has been so enlightening for me. Through your gentle prodding and guidance I was able to write a speech that connects with the audience. I wish everyone could experience the transformation I have undergone. You have helped me discover the warm and compelling stories that now make my speech reach hearts and uplift minds. This was truly an empowering experience. I cannot thank you enough for your great assistance." — J.S.

"Tom Marcoux has been an NAB Conference favorite [speaker] for six years. And he is very energetic."
– John Marino,
Vice President, National Association of Broadcasters, Washington, D.C.

"Using just one of Tom Marcoux's methods, I got more done in 2 weeks than in 6 months."
– Jaclyn Freitas, M.A.

Tom's Coaching features innovations:
- Dynamic Rehearsal
- Power Rehearsal for Crisis

- The Charisma Advantage that Saves Time

Become a fan of Tom's graphic novels/feature films:
Fantasy Thriller: *Jack AngelSword*
type "JackAngelSword" at Facebook.com
Science fiction: *TimePulse*
www.facebook.com/timepulsegraphicnovel

Children's Fantasy: *Crystal Pegasus*
www.facebook.com/crystalpegasusandrose
See **Free Chapters** of Tom Marcoux's 24 books at http://amzn.to/ZiCTRj

Special Offer Just for Readers of this Book:
Contact Tom Marcoux at tomsupercoach@gmail.com for special discounts on books, coaching, workshops and presentations. Just mention your experience with this book.

www.ingramcontent.com/pod-product-compliance
Lightning Source LLC
Chambersburg PA
CBHW071308110426
42743CB00042B/1216